Traveling the World in the 1960s and 70s

By Ship, Train, Bus, Plane
& Sometimes Hitchhiking

Walt Christophersen

Copyright 2011 by Walt Christophersen

2020 Edition

All rights reserved. No part of this publication may be reproduced, stored in a retrieval system or transmitted in any form or by any means, electronic, mechanical, photocopying, recording or otherwise, without prior written permission of the author, except by a reviewer who may quote brief passages.

ISBN 978-0-9837235-0-9

Back cover portrait by David Schmidt, Phoenix

Buckeroo Books
Arizona USA
E-mail: eurobook@q.com

Contents

The real Pacific   1
Getting swamped • Marshall Islands footnotes • Field Trip I • Ponape footnotes • Truk footnotes • Guam footnotes • Yap footnotes • Palau footnotes • Field Trip II • The finale

South Pacific   33
Tahiti and the golden letter • Circling Tahiti by thumb • The 'dangerous islands' • Tahiti's sister island • Bali Ha'i is calling • The Samoas: divided by history • Feasting in the last Polynesian kingdom • Fiji and the girls of Vanua Vatu • French accent • New Zealand, quickly • Australia coast-to-coast • The rock • The road north • Penguins & other creatures

South America   79
Sailing down the Amazon • Amazon footnotes • Traveling companions • Rio! • Striking out • Tierra del Fuego • Riding the rails to Lake Titicaca

Norway   109
A cruise that went somewhere

The beginnings   117
Inspiration • Europe welcomes the lower classes • Setting foot in Europe • Living like the Brits • Bedbugs & Sara • A lift in Spain • Hostelling • Rules of the road • Back roads of Algeria • A small town in Macedonia

Asian odyssey   133
Taking a break • The Alexandria scam • Valley of the Kings • Working, briefly • By bus to Baghdad • U-Turn on the river • Bumpy road to Afghanistan • Kabul and the Khyber Restaurant • Long day at the airport • Adjusting to India • Shocking Agra • New Year's in Bombay • Hot and grubby Madras • Oh, Calcutta! • Packed like sardines • Refreshing Nepal • Two wild and crazy guys • Burmese days • Bangkok: Oriental LA • Detour to Vientiane • The bus to Angkor • Stranded in Saigon • To Singapore by train and taxi • Slightly upriver in Borneo • Brunei and Labuan • The visa/ticket dilemma • Bunking with the Peace Corps • Amazing coincidence • At home on the Star Ferry • Pizzas in Taiwan • Slipping and sliding to Japan • Hitching to Tokyo • Home at last • Footnote

The real Pacific

Getting swamped

    The sea was choppy as a heavily loaded boat with nine people aboard left the beach and bounced through the surf at an island called Faraulep, heading for a ship drifting off the coast.
    It was late afternoon. Rain made the water look gray and put a chill in the air.
    As the driver gunned the outboard motor, the 16-foot boat was hammered by the waves. One man went flying overboard. Other passengers quickly pulled him in.
    The swells were running four feet high as the small wooden boat drew alongside the ship. Grabbing the swinging rope ladder was tricky. One man trying to climb aboard lost his footing and fell into the sea. But he managed to get a grip on the ladder and pull himself up.

    It was day 15 of a field trip through the outer islands of Yap in the western Pacific. People were returning to the ship at the end of a daylong stop at the island.
    After the shore boat arrived for the final time and the last few passengers were scampering up the ladder, a big swell flipped it over. Drenched crewmen righted the boat and hooked a cable to the bow so it could be hoisted aboard.

    I was the guy who slipped off the ladder.
    It was January of 1971 and I was getting my first taste of the Pacific on a trip through Micronesia, a vast area between Hawaii and the Philippines that had remained virtually untouched by commercial tourism.

I was a freelance travel writer at the time, contributing articles and photographs to a number of Sunday newspapers. My experiences in the islands were summarized in a two part report:

Micronesia
South Seas without Ruffles

How do you like your islands?

If you're willing to sacrifice the luxuries of Hawaii and Tahiti for the thrill of discovering the real Pacific, then just change planes in Honolulu and head west until you reach Micronesia.

Here, in a patch of ocean as large as the United States, you'll find plenty of islands that haven't changed much since the days Melville, Maugham and James Norman Hall sailed the Pacific.

Micronesia means "little islands" – a well-chosen title. There are more than 2,100 of them, but they're so small you could lump them all inside that reliable old comparative Rhode Island and have lots of surfing space left over.

Located just north of the Equator, Micronesia would certainly fit anyone's concept of the fabled South Seas.

Consider these diversions. Swimmers can collect sea shells along an untouched coral reef or flirt with angelfish while exploring the mysteries of a barnacle-encrusted shipwreck at the bottom of an emerald lagoon.

Landlubbers can soak up the sun on a deserted white beach, climb into the cockpit of a Japanese Zero that was peppered in an air raid in 1944 or maybe visit an isolated island inhabited by happy people who have never seen a telephone or an ice cream cone.

Tourists may still be a novelty here but in the past Micronesia played host to an odd variety of visitors including planters, missionaries, whalers, blackbirders (slave traders) and assorted scoundrels.

The islands changed hands three times in the past 74 years – each time as spoils of war. The Spanish, who moved in during the late 1600s, sold out to the Germans after losing the Spanish-American War in 1898. The League of Nations gave the islands to Japan following Germany's defeat in the First World War. The Japanese broke their lease at Pearl Harbor.

Most of Micronesia (except for Guam and some British possessions) is now officially known as the U.S. Trust Territory of the Pacific Islands, a designation dating from 1947 when the U.N. granted landlord status to the United States. The Trust Territory – or TT as it's called – consists of six districts.

The Marianas and the Marshalls each constitute a district in themselves. The Caroline Islands are divided into four districts: Ponape, Truk, Yap and Palau. The TT's administrative headquarters is on the island of Saipan in the Marianas.

Each district has at least one language of its own, in addition to English, and a slightly different culture. Total population is about 100,000.

The geography ranges from lush mountainous islands in the west to dry low-lying atolls – small islands perched on circular coral reefs – in the east.

Strict security kept tourists out of Micronesia during the Japanese and early

American administrations, but now the area is virtually wide open and, thanks to a fairly new air service, more accessible than ever.

Air Micronesia, a subsidiary of Continental, has two island-hopping jet flights a week between Honolulu and Saipan. The fare is comparatively low. You can fly all the way to Palau for less than it costs to get to Tahiti, which is half as far from the U.S. mainland.

Since the TT is under U.S. control, Americans can stay for as long as 30 days without a passport or visa. Those who wish to linger awhile need an entry permit.

The eastern gateway to Micronesia is Majuro, an atoll that serves as the district center for the Marshall Islands.

Majuro's main island is a crescent-shaped sliver of sand and palm trees about 30 miles long. It used to be a chain of islands until the U.S. Navy filled in the empty spaces to build a road – or, more accurately, a 30-mile string of potholes.

Majuro is short on tourist attractions, the chief point of interest being a village at the far end of the road. The "downtown" area resembles the other district centers in that it's a conglomeration of new houses and stores mixed in with weathered quonset huts and shacks made from old shipping crates.

The next district center to the west is Ponape, a jungle-covered island with mountain peaks that poke through the clouds to a height of 2,500 feet. Ponape is known for its ancient ruins and boisterous bars.

The ruins are those of Nan Madol, a city built of volcanic rock some 700 years ago. It's located across the island from the main town of Kolonia, but due to a lack of roads, it can be reached only by sea. Tours cost $25 per boatload and the trip takes 90 minutes each way.

Ponape is the drinking capital of Micronesia. Kolonia boasts 15 bars – one for every 230 men, women and children. To the distress of many Ponapeans, all bars were temporarily closed a few months ago following a shootout between imbibers and police.

A footnote on lawbreaking: it isn't uncommon in any district center to see a small work detail of convicts cutting grass with machetes. Their guard is always a policeman armed with only a billy club.

In the Truk district, the main island is Moen. The name Truk refers to the 40-mile-wide lagoon that surrounds Moen and nearly a dozen other large islands.

Truk is a scuba diver's heaven. The Japanese used the lagoon as a naval stronghold until American bombers neutralized it by sinking an estimated 60 warships.

To get to the rest of Micronesia, you must pass through Guam, a full-fledged U.S. property with no political ties to the TT. In addition to being the economic hub of the western Pacific, Guam has a number of good hotels and restaurants that attract thousands of vacationers and honeymooners from Japan each year.

North of Guam is Saipan, a familiar name from World War Two. Saipan has the finest beaches of all the district centers and is one of the few islands in the trust area with paved roads. War relics include a Japanese command post and a crumbling prison where some people believe Amelia Earhart was held.

Yap and Palau are linked to Guam by DC-6 flights.

Yap – the home of stone money and topless women – is undeniably the most interesting part of Micronesia, probably because it best fits our idea of what the South Seas should be like.

The stone money is easy to find but the bare-breasted women are becoming more elusive as Yap grudgingly yields to progress. Although many Yapese men still prefer loincloths to trousers, most women don blouses before venturing into the district center, Colonia, to do their shopping.

Yap's airport is a treat for war buffs. The remains of more than a dozen Zeros are scattered about the area.

In Palau, the rock islands are the main attraction. These geological oddities are dome-shaped masses of rock blanketed with thick vegetation. Hundreds of them, many resembling giant green mushrooms, dot the lagoon between the district center of Koror and the island of Peliliu.

Peliliu, the scene of a two month battle during the war, is a living museum. The concrete shells of a Japanese navy barracks and a communications center are still standing. Half-sunken landing craft in the harbor and tanks in the jungle sit where they were when the fighting ended.

The hotels in Micronesia range in quality from deluxe to barely habitable. Half were built within the past two or three years.

Room rates run from $4.50 for a

shared bath single at the Kaselehlia Inn in Ponape to $28 for a plush double at the Continental Travelodge in Truk.

The most unique hotel is the Ponape in Ponape, where guests stay in modern thatched huts with private bath for $12 double. It's located in a Polynesian village out of town.

The worst hotel has to be the very plain MIECO (Marshall Islands Import-Export Company) in Majuro. The minimum tab of $7.50 includes running water several times a day and candles for use when the electricity goes out.

Bring along plenty of mosquito repellent. Despite a lack of tropical diseases, the mosquitoes have gluttonous appetites.

The TT government has prepared an excellent guidebook loaded with useful information on all the district centers. Ask for it at any Continental Airlines office or write: Office of Tourism, Trust Territory of the Pacific Islands, Saipan, Mariana Islands 96950. Yes, each district has its own Zip Code.

The real adventure in Micronesia begins when you step onto a ship for a visit to the untouristed outer islands.

Micronesia's Outer Islands
Don't Step on Any Starfish

Any adventurous soul who has more time than money and doesn't mind roughing it a bit can visit the unspoiled outer islands of Micronesia by hopping on one of the government ships based in each of the six district centers.

There are a dozen such ships whose goal is to call at every one of the 90-some inhabited outer islands at least once a month. The average voyage, or field trip, lasts about two weeks and covers six to eight atolls and islands.

Each voyage has a threefold purpose: to carry passengers, transport round trip government employees who tend to the needs of the islanders, and unload food and supplies in exchange for copra (dried coconut meat used for making products such as soap, margarine and nitroglycerine).

Most of the ships are around 150 feet in length. The larger ones have space for as many as 20 cabin passengers. Nearly all the bunks are filled by government people, a doctor, representatives of the local trading company and a few Peace Corps volunteers.

Fares are based on the number of miles in a straight line from the home port to the most distant island on the itinerary. Cabin passengers pay four cents per mile, plus a $1 a day bunk fee. Meals cost another $5 per day.

I spent two weeks sailing the Marshalls for $37.40 and three weeks in the outer islands of Yap for $56.60, not including meals.

One of the first things I learned from the old-timers was that it was wise to carry your own food because you can eat much better at half the ship's price. The cooks tend to favor corned beef with rice, even before the chicken runs out.

You also must be prepared for bad plumbing, rationed shower water and a complete lack of privacy – roommates can be of either sex. But despite all the drawbacks, it's worth it.

Yap and the Marshalls are decades apart in development.

The Marshallese have adopted more Western ways because of a deeper exposure to foreign influence and a lack of natural resources. They have a strange affinity for corrugated metal roofs. Many have forsaken their outriggers for factory-built boats with 20-horsepower engines. They rely on the field trip ships for a good deal of their food and clothing. Men wear shirts and slacks while women prefer muumuus or simple cotton dresses.

The conservative Yapese enjoy life the way it is and see no reason to rush into the 20th Century. They still roof their homes with palm fronds, build sturdy sailing canoes without the use of nails and refuse to abandon their traditional attire: loincloths for men, *lava-lavas* for women and grass skirts for girls.

Some of the *lava-lavas*, or knee-length skirts, are store-bought. Others are made by the women on looms.

The most unusual experience of the Yap field trip was a five-day stop at Lamotrek, where chiefs from all over the district gathered to hold an annual conference.

The women pooled their efforts to make leis and fix meals for the chiefs and other visitors. After a concluding dinner featuring sea turtle, pork and tuna, guests were entertained with songs by the young women of the island.

The ship used on that trip was the 178-foot M/V *Ran Annim* (a Trukese greeting similar to aloha). Two steel chambers erected on the fantail served as cabins, each containing 10 bunks. In addition to the usual passengers, there were two American professors from the University of Guam, two Swedish medical students and the Yap elementary school superintendent, an American who brought along his fearless wife and two young children.

The worst part of the voyage was when the showers were shut off for 12 days to conserve water. People got so grubby that when the ship hit a rain squall everyone ran onto the deck with a bar of soap for a mass cleansing.

In the Marshalls, I sailed on the M/V *Militobi*, a ship named after the eastern and westernmost islands of Micronesia. The 158-foot *Militobi* was considered one of the better ships with 18 bunks divided among five cabins.

I was assigned to a four-bunk cabin equipped with two closets and a functioning cold water wash basin. It had about as much floor space as three phone booths. My roommates were a Marshallese public works official, a young American employed by the school system and a Peace Corps girl.

There were two showers down the hall that ran for one hour each day.

The only other fare-paying cabin passengers besides me were the elderly wife of a Majuro-based missionary and her visiting daughter, a freelance writer who specialized in marine biology. They were lucky enough to have their own cabin.

Since the ship was sailing north from Majuro, the captain opted to take on water and fuel at Kwajalein, a U.S. missile base that was technically off-limits to tourists. Air travelers arriving at Kwajalein were confined to the terminal unless they had business on the island. Every American aboard the *Militobi*, however, was permitted ashore with no questions asked.

The military end of the island bristled with towers and domes, making it look like Expo '67 from the sea. In the residential section, the architecture was U.S. Army Modern: rows and rows of cinderblock houses with well-trimmed lawns and a rat guard on every palm tree.

Kwajalein's well-stocked stores, with their low PX prices, were ideal places to pick up field trip supplies.

The first outer island we stopped at, Likiep, held a real surprise – a large house built by a Portuguese trader around the turn of the century. It stood about five feet off the ground on heavy stilts, had three rooms and was surrounded by a wide veranda.

Although the house was generally dilapidated, the people maintained the sitting room as it was 50 years earlier. A chandelier hung directly over a circular table and four outsized chairs. In one corner was a roll-top desk, its veneer cracked and peeling from the humidity. There was even a pedal-powered

Singer sewing machine. Decorations included a ship in a bottle and a brass sextant encased in glass.

The effect was enthralling. You could almost picture the trader standing on his veranda in a rumpled white linen suit, inviting a visitor to join him for a gin and tonic while joking about a lack of ice.

Another interesting port of call for the *Militobi* was Wotje, a former key Japanese military base.

Wotje must have been a bustling place before the war. Jutting into the lagoon was a concrete wharf with a toppled steel crane at the end. There were pillboxes along the beach to defend an airstrip, oil storage tanks and a miniature railroad. Interspersed among the islanders' houses were the remains of half a dozen reinforced concrete buildings including an ice house. You had to look hard to find one square foot of concrete that wasn't pitted by an American bullet.

Like most of the dots on a map of Micronesia, both Wotje and Likiep are atolls. An atoll can include any number of islands. Often only one is inhabited, sometimes two. Population can vary between 50 and 300. The larger islands may be no larger than a couple of city blocks.

When calling at an atoll, the ships anchor in the lagoon, providing there's a gap in the reef large enough to squeeze through. Passengers are taken ashore in one of the ship's 14-foot boats, which they board by climbing down a rope ladder.

Getting ashore at the island of Mejit was especially tricky because there's no lagoon to speak of. Mejit is a single island surrounded by a reef that comes practically right up to the beach. It's not one of those fragile coral reefs with colorful fish dashing about; it's more like a solid hunk of concrete.

The reef sits so high that its outer edge acts as a breakwater at low tide. Even an unloaded boat can't clear it. As a result, passengers have to jump from the boat to the reef, then walk ashore.

Timing is important. When the boat reaches the reef, the bow line is tossed to waiting islanders. They tug on it as the driver reverses the engine to hold the boat perpendicular to the reef. Each passenger must jump just as a breaking wave hurls the boat against the reef. He has one second to make his move before the boat slips back and the receding sea spills off the reef like a waterfall.

It's a different story at high tide when the boat barely clears the reef. As soon as it gets on the reef, everyone gets out and pushes it forward each time a wave temporarily floats it. Tennis shoes are handy for walking across the Mejit reef, which has a rough texture. You have to watch for holes and be careful you don't step on any starfish.

The length of time a ship spends at each island depends primarily on how much copra is to be loaded. It can take anywhere from several hours to two days.

Sailing dates, which can be obtained by writing to the district administrator, are subject to change for a number of reasons. It would be rare if a ship actually sailed when scheduled.

On the *Militobi*, our return was delayed by a medical emergency. The ship was heading for home when headquarters diverted us to an island named Ailinglapalap to pick up a women suffering from a broken arm and possible internal injuries. It seems she was the victim of progress – she had been run over by the only motor scooter on the island.

My journey through Micronesia stretched over two months, beginning December 3, 1970 and ending January 28, 1971.

The articles got good play, appearing in the *Los Angeles Times, San Francisco Examiner, Boston Globe* and *Toronto Star* – papers that regularly published my work. Even the usually snobbish *Washington Post* printed them.

Although the pieces were much longer than usual, there were many things I had to omit, such as …

The "little islands" of Micronesia make up one of three ethnic areas in the Pacific. The largest is Polynesia, which means "many islands." It stretches from Hawaii in the north to Easter Island in the southeast and all the way west to New Zealand. There's also Melanesia or "black islands," which covers an area between New Guinea and Fiji.

As I hopped across the Pacific, I could see the appearance of the islanders change gradually as they became less Polynesian and more Melanesian.

Marshall Islands footnotes

Majuro, the eastern gateway to the islands, was reached by a five-hour flight aboard an Air Micronesia 727 out of Honolulu, a trip that included a brief refueling stop at Johnston Island.

Majuro wasn't the best introduction to Micronesia. Too many buildings were made of corrugated metal, there was some garbage floating in the lagoon and the land was as low and flat as could be.

I had read about the field trip ships but had no idea when one might be sailing. I was incredibly lucky because I arrived to find one was leaving the very next day. There was just enough time to buy a ticket and get Trust Territory approval to climb aboard.

Field Trip I

The *Militobi* was one of three ships making the voyage on a rotating basis in the Marshalls.

At each stop, the ships took aboard copra while selling goods to the islanders, goods that could include anything from sugar and rice and clothing to lumber and bags of cement.

Copra is made by husking a coconut, then chopping the shell in half with a machete and drying the meat in the sun. After that, the meat is packed in burlap sacks, weighed – usually on a portable scale suspended from a pole – then hauled to the ship in one of the small boats. A heavy rope net is spread across the inside of the boats before the copra bags are tossed in so they can be winched into the ship's hold. At the time, copra sold for $102 to $105 a ton.

The islanders usually traveled as deck passengers unless they were officials. Most of them congregated on the hatch covers in the middle of the ship, an area covered by tarps to shield them from the sun.

Passengers such as me were permitted to go ashore whenever there was room in the boat. Naturally, preference was given to local people and cargo. Once ashore, visitors would talk with the islanders, take pictures, explore the island and maybe go swimming.

Arrivals and departures depended on variables such as the weather and tides, the amount of time it took to load or unload cargo and how long it would take to sail to the next island.

Since in-transit air travelers weren't allowed out of the terminal at Kwajalein and journalists reportedly were banned from the island, I was fortunate to get ashore and roam around. After all, it was a hush-hush U.S. military base where missiles were fired to intercept rockets launched from Vandenberg Air Force Base in Southern California. Of course I was interested not in the missiles but the Surfway supermarket, where I stocked up for the trip.

There was also a laundromat and a snack bar, two things I would have appreciated much more at the end of the trip when I was tired and grubby.

Kwajalein was like a country club. A couple of thousand Americans lived there, and they were provided with plenty of amenities and diversions to keep them from going crazy in the middle of the ocean. Think of Kwajalein as a small American town that had almost everything you could possibly want, except you were surrounded by water and couldn't go anywhere unless you got on a boat or plane.

The contrast between Kwajalein and the island of Ebeye, three miles away, was remarkable. Ebeye was packed with Marshallese islanders and their extended families, many of whom worked at the base and commuted by boat.

Ebeye was regarded as one of the most crowded spots on Earth. In fact, some people called it a slum. Reliable population figures were hard to come by. Let's just say Ebeye had considerably more residents than Kwajalein living in a small fraction of the space.

Kwajalein is one of the largest atolls in the Pacific. The lagoon measures 66 miles long by 18 wide, providing an excellent anchorage for countless ships. Although the atoll is formed by a string of at least 90 islands of all sizes, if lumped together they wouldn't amount to much – a total of little more than six square miles.

At the other extreme, islands such as Mejit sit alone and isolated, with a narrow lagoon ringed by a reef.

In some cases, a lagoon might be too shallow to accommodate a ship. Or it could be deep enough but there might not be a large enough opening in the reef.

Research on the old house on Likiep showed it was built around 1905 by Joachim deBrum, son of a Portuguese trader named José deBrum. Both José and a German named Adolph Capelle had been sailing around the Pacific in the mid-1800s. They eventually wound up together on Likiep, married Marshallese women and started a successful copra trading business.

The house was constructed largely of California redwood planks that were transported across the Pacific lashed to the sides of ships because they were too long to fit on deck.

DeBrum assembled an extensive library as well as a photographic studio. He left behind nearly 2,500 glass plate negatives that were protected during World War Two by burying them on a smaller island.

When I was there, it appeared deBrum's property was largely being ignored. There were several outer buildings that could hardly be seen due to overgrown vegetation. However, everything has since been spruced up. In 2010, the Portuguese government chipped in $70,000 to help with the upkeep.

Snorkeling possibilities are endless in Micronesia. There's an incredible amount of marine life waiting to be seen in as little as two or three feet of crystal clear lagoon water.

It helped that the missionary's daughter on the *Militobi,* Bonnie Jean McNiel of Walla Walla, Washington, was an expert on marine life. She tipped me off about what to watch for underwater as well as what to watch out for.

Simply sticking my head underwater was like peering into a tropical aquarium. It was fascinating to see clown fish thread their way through the tentacles of sea anemones. The clown fish is the bright orange fish with white rings that gained fame in the Disney film, *Finding Nemo.* It's immune to the poison the anemones use to kill other creatures.

In my article, I cautioned against stepping on starfish. That was to protect the starfish. A real danger is the sea urchin, a black, golf ball-sized creature with detachable spines that can get stuck, very painfully like fishhooks, in a person's foot. There are plenty of them. That's why it's wise to wear tennis shoes when swimming if one doesn't have flippers.

There was a lot of downtime while sailing across the open sea between islands. For example, it took 24 ½ hours to get from Majuro to Kwajalein.

If I wasn't lounging on deck, talking with someone or washing clothes when the water came on, I did a lot of reading. On the *Militobi,* I tore through three books I had brought with me, plus four *Reader's Digests, Life, Argosy* and anything else with print on paper. I even devoured Seventh Day Adventist literature carried by the missionary's wife.

Although most days at sea were uneventful, the weather livened things up occasionally. Heading for the island of Ailuk, it was so rough that anything not stowed properly became airborne and crashed to the deck. That included some food jars Bonnie Jean and her mother had in their cabin.

Following the field trip, I was flying out of Kwajalein but wasn't permitted to stay there overnight, so I checked into a hotel in Ebeye. There was a movie theater in the same building and I could hear the sound clearly as I went to bed, but I was so tired I fell asleep anyway.

Ponape footnotes

One and a half hours by air from Kwajalein, Ponape was totally different. Whereas the highest spot in the Marshalls was only 33 feet (on Likiep), Ponape – as noted in the article – had peaks as high as 2,500 feet.

It was also one of the rainiest places on Earth, with as much as 300 inches per year. Forty rivers carried water to the sea. In contrast, the annual average rainfall in some of the Marshalls was only 20 inches, forcing people to capture and store rainwater in large concrete tanks.

With a circumference of 80 miles, Ponape was one of the larger islands of Micronesia. The main town was Kolonia.

Immediately upon arriving, I discovered that a large ship was about to sail for the island of Kusaie, nearly 300 miles to the southeast.

Kusaie is a high island favored by scuba divers for its pristine coral reefs. It had a turbulent history punctuated by the arrival of a number of outsiders, notably strict Boston missionaries in 1862 and a notorious Cleveland-born pirate named Bully Hayes in the 1870s. In their book, *Rascals in Paradise,* James Michener and A. Grove Day said Hayes was so infamous that "his name was whispered at night on lonely atolls to scare children."

Although the thought of sailing was tempting, I convinced myself not to jump aboard every ship that came along, especially since I had just spent two weeks at sea.

For visitors to Ponape wanting a glimpse of Polynesia without boarding a ship, there was a village on the edge of Kolonia called Porakied that was home to several hundred transplants from Kapingamarangi.

Located 450 miles to the southwest, Kapingamarangi is one of two atolls in Micronesia populated by ethnic Polynesians. The other is Nukuoro. The transplants wore wrap-around *lava-lavas* and built their homes and sleek fishing boats Polynesian-style.

A guidebook said there was a nice waterfall about half an hour's walk from the end of a road outside Kolonia. I took a taxi to the jumping off spot and discovered the hike was more like three hours. After one hour on an old road and a path through the rain forest, it was a two hour trek up the middle of a stream – a wet and rocky staircase.

On the way up, I slipped and hurt my left middle toe. I eventually made it to a waterfall, although it may not have been the one I had set out to find. In any case, it was nice.

A doctor back in town told me my toe was probably broken. He said I could either have a metal pin inserted – but not there – or leave it alone and it would heal in six to eight weeks. I left it alone and walked carefully for a while.

Two days before Christmas, Santa Claus turned up in Kolonia. Ponapean kids gathered in a ballpark to watch him arrive by helicopter. Santa and his two assistants were actually U.S. Navy Seabees who handed out candy and Christmas stockings.

Truk footnotes

Like Kwajalein, Truk has one of the largest lagoons in the Pacific with 11 principal islands sheltered inside a necklace of scores of islets. The lagoon covers an area of 833 square miles. No wonder it was a key Japanese naval base.

U.S. forces attacked Truk on February 17, 1944. Waves of carrier-based aircraft pounded the area for two days, destroying 200 Japanese planes on the ground and sinking 41 ships. A follow-up raid 10 weeks later finished the job and took Truk completely out of the war.

Today the entire lagoon is classified as a monument, meaning nothing can be removed without permission. Not surprisingly, diving tourism is a major business. Shipwrecks can be found at depths ranging from six to 230 feet.

I arrived in Truk on a very quiet Christmas Eve and went with a guy at the airport who was shilling for the Maramar Hotel, not far away, where I got a room.

Although nothing was moving on Christmas Day, I started walking and ran into Mike and Sue Cozad, a 20-something brother and sister who were living on Truk while their father supervised the construction of a hotel. They invited me to join them in their beat up Volkswagen Beetle to search for remnants of the Japanese occupation.

We found guns poking out of caves and visited a lighthouse on one corner of the island.

Later we headed for the Continental Hotel, located on a beach a short distance out of town, planning to have Christmas dinner, only to learn the hotel had neither food nor water. So we went to their place where their father fixed ham, peas and potatoes on a hot plate.

The day after Christmas was a Saturday. It was raining and promised to be an all day downpour. Nevertheless, I walked around town staying under cover as much as possible. There wasn't much there other than a number of quonset huts. Activity revolved around a general store called the Truk Trading Company.

I ran into Mike again and we arranged to visit the nearby island of Dublon the next day. Dublon had been the Japanese district headquarters and there were extensive ruins there. More than 40,000 Japanese had lived in Truk leading up to the war.

We got lucky and split the cost of a boat with two Japanese men who wanted to go fishing. It was ironic that they had no interest in the ruins when other Japanese traveled to Micronesia specifically to visit sites associated with the war.

On the way to Dublon, we stopped for an hour at a smaller island called Eten, a onetime fighter plane base. There wasn't much left of the airstrip, but there were two Zeros under only a couple of feet of water at one end of the island.

On Dublon, while the Japanese fished, Mike and I

explored what was left of a large hospital and numerous fortifications in the area.

A popular souvenir in Truk was the lovestick – a long, thin piece of wood like a conductor's baton with unique carvings on it.

In the old days, each young man would carve his own designs on a stick and familiarize his girlfriend with it. At night, when she was sleeping with the rest of her family inside their thatched hut, the guy would slide the stick through the wall and poke her with it. After she felt it to verify who the owner was, she would slip out to join him.

Guam footnotes

An hour and 20 minutes from Truk, Guam was little more than a pit stop on the way to Yap, a place to check for mail and hit the Dairy Queen and the laundromat.

With huge hotels lining the beach, the capital, Agana, looked like a mini Honolulu. It was nice to be back in the world for two days.

Yap footnotes

The district center of Yap was Colonia. A DC-6 flew there from Guam in two hours.

At the airport, a waiting bus took passengers to the only hotel in town, the 10-room Rai View. I was put in a double room with a young Japanese guy. The bathroom was down the hall. Fresh from air conditioned Guam, the noisy ceiling fan reminded me I was still in the tropics.

After checking in, I walked back to the airport to look over aircraft destroyed during the war. The airport had been a

Japanese base and there were quite a few Zeros as well as some heavy bombers littering the area.

Downtown Colonia consisted mainly of the hotel, the Yap Cooperative Association, which was a general store, and O'Keefe's Oasis, one of several bars in town – a good place to get cheeseburgers, fries and a beer.

The Oasis was named for Captain David O'Keefe, an enterprising Irish buccaneer who became rich and powerful in the 1870s by hauling stone money to Yap from quarries in Palau, 300 miles to the west. The Yapese had been transporting the money for centuries, but many lives were lost when their overloaded boats capsized on the way home. O'Keefe stepped in with his ship to perform a valuable public service.

After living like royalty in Yap for years, he set off on a voyage in 1901 and was never seen again, presumably lost at sea. His adventures formed the basis of a 1954 film called *His Majesty O'Keefe*, starring Burt Lancaster. It can sometimes be seen on Turner Classic Movies.

Each piece of stone money has a hole in the middle so it can be carried on a pole, although toting the larger pieces would require more than muscle power. The money can still be seen all around the district center, which is comprised of four islands.

There are at least 10,000 pieces propped up here and there, the largest measuring about 14 feet in diameter. The weathered coins might appear to be abandoned, but everyone knows who owns each piece, and even if one changes hands, it isn't necessarily moved.

New Year's Day, 1971, dawned two days after I arrived in Yap, but I missed New Year's Eve. I was so tired from walking that not even the roar of people celebrating at O'Keefe's could keep me awake until midnight.

I planned to sail aboard a field trip ship to the outer islands. After learning it wasn't leaving for a few days, I decided to make a quick trip to Palau that same day.

Palau footnotes

My Japanese roommate was also going to Palau, so we traveled together.

After a one hour flight, we landed on a large island called Babelthuap. The building serving as the air terminal was a battered Japanese communications center left over from the war. We were put on a bus headed to the district center, Koror. Part of the ride had us traveling across a strait on a cable-guided ferryboat.

The bus dropped us at the Royal Palauan Hotel and we got a room together. Actually, it was two adjoining rooms, so we each had a lot of space.

Since we both wanted to see the war-ravaged island of Peliliu, we tracked down a boat and arranged a charter for the next morning.

Peliliu, which occupies only five square miles of land, lies at the tip of a 25-mile-long lagoon stretching south from Koror. Getting there took us right through Palau's number one scenic attraction, the rock islands, where the Yap stone money was quarried.

Once at Peliliu, we found a man who took us around in his jeep for a small fee. I was surprised to see so much war debris. At one beach, there were several wrecked American landing craft jutting through the surf, halted just yards from shore. I also saw two shattered Japanese tanks, one U.S. tank and the remains of a plane that had nosedived into the trees.

At one point, my roommate stopped at a Japanese shrine to meditate or say a prayer, indicating he may have known someone who fought there. I didn't ask.

Walking through the underbrush, I spotted an American steel helmet and a canteen cup. On the side of the cup, someone had scratched "06/06/1944" – D-Day at Normandy – presumably an inspiration for the troops.

The claw-shaped island was the scene of one of the bloodiest battles of the Pacific. Fighting raged from September

15 to November 27, 1944, and the casualty rate was the highest for any amphibious landing in the Pacific. The most conservative figures show at least 1,500 American Marines and soldiers killed and nearly 6,300 wounded.

Japanese forces were literally annihilated. Of the 10,900 combat troops on the island, one source claimed only 19 survived.

In his *Time-Life* book, *Island Fighting*, Rafael Steinberg noted that the Japanese were dug in so well that "it took an average of 1,589 rounds of heavy and light ammunition" to kill each one.

Even today, there remains plenty of war debris on the island, including potentially dangerous explosives.

I often get a spooky feeling at battlefields, as if ghosts might be lurking about. That feeling was never stronger than at Peliliu.

Field Trip II

Before boarding the *Ran Annim* on January 5, I bought $32 worth of food, most at the Yap Cooperative Association. I also took what I expected to be my last shower for a while, then joined some Peace Corps volunteers at O'Keefe's for cheeseburgers and a couple of beers.

Once aboard the ship, I found that eight of the 10 bunks in my cabin were taken, mostly by Americans. There were two identical cabins on the rear deck and they looked as if they'd been built as an afterthought, not original equipment.

There was one tiny combination toilet/shower with no lock on the door. The shower water was to be turned on each day between 6 and 7 a.m. and p.m.

The first island we stopped at was Ulithi, home of the Outer Islands High School. Most of the houses were built of rusty metal – not very picturesque.

The second stop, Fais, was one of those islands where the ship couldn't enter the lagoon, so we drifted offshore while small boats ferried people and goods back and forth. Since one end of the island had sheer rock cliffs, the shore boats had to land at a beach where waves breaking from two directions crashed together. Getting splashed was unavoidable.

Among the interesting things to see ashore were the remains of a Japanese railway used to transport phosphate.

Sorol was another island that was hard to approach, but the ship visited even though only seven families lived there.

The population on any island or atoll is limited by the availability of fresh water as well as how much food can be procured from both the land and sea. Islanders have occasionally been forced to move elsewhere when their home atoll couldn't sustain them.

Despite heavy seas on occasion, I never saw anyone get seasick. After all, most of the people on the ship had grown up surrounded by water.

Just the threat of bad weather kept us anchored in the lagoon at Woleai an extra day. When the Filipino captain heard a typhoon might be brewing elsewhere in the islands, he decided to stay put. Another time, he sailed off course for a few hours to avoid rough seas.

The American doctor making his rounds by ship was Joseph "Jay" Gutenkauf, a sandy-haired, bespectacled guy from Minnesota. He traveled light. In addition to carrying an eye chart and lenses for vision tests, his dental kit consisted solely of syringes for administering Novocain and a forceps for pulling teeth.

On one island, I noticed what looked like a cage in the middle of the village. It was made of long poles about three inches in diameter pounded into the ground, forming a square measuring about six by six feet.

I asked what it was for. I was told there was a man who went a little crazy now and then. The villagers put him in the cage until he calmed down.

If true, that cage was the local mental health clinic.

The two professors from Guam were Bruce Karolle and Marvin Montvel-Cohen. Bruce was the guy who fell out of the boat leaving Faraulep.

They had devised a no hassle menu, bringing aboard a few cases of canned tuna and a tin of ship's biscuits. The biscuits, sometimes known as hardtack, are a hefty version of a saltine cracker minus the salt. They measure about three inches square and at least ¼ inch thick, are more solid than flaky and come in a tin about one foot high and nine inches square.

After eating nothing but tuna and biscuits for more than a week, the professors were getting desperate and willing to trade for almost anything. I got to sample the tuna/biscuit cuisine in exchange for a can of spaghetti.

As mentioned in the article, meals provided by the ship not only added $5 a day to the trip, but they got boring fast. For each trip, I brought along a wide variety of canned goods plus Carnation Instant Breakfast, Tang, Coke, beer and other nonperishable items – enough for at least one and a half meals each day. Spaghetti was by far my number one canned item, followed by vegetables, tuna and little hot dogs.

Island food is an acquired taste. The main staple is taro, which is used to make the Hawaiian dish known as poi. It's a tuber-type plant that tastes like modeling clay, even when mashed and flavored with coconut milk.

If conditions are right, a village usually has a taro patch out back, a swampy area where the plant is cultivated. When taro is needed, a woman will wade knee-deep into the patch – never a man – pull out a plant by the leaves, lop the root off with a machete, then replace the upper part, which will grow another root.

Breadfruit isn't bad. Slices can be cooked like French fries on a piece of tin over a fire.

For the islanders, two items that top the gourmet list are Spam and Argentine canned corned beef.

One evening on Lamotrek, about a dozen men were sitting in a circle passing around bottles of what was called *tuba* – a wine made from fermented sap of the coconut tree. They invited me to sample it.

Tuba is milky white. It's prepared in huge Japanese soy sauce bottles. There were many bottles placed in the middle of the circle. One at a time, each was passed from man to man with a single glass from which to drink, always with a quick gulp. After drinking, the custom was to turn the glass upside down and shake the remaining drops onto the ground.

The taste was hard to describe, sort of like coconut milk laced with some kind of anesthetic. I don't know how it affected anyone else, but I was groggy after a few glasses – certainly not a pleasant feeling.

The American couple with two kids was Ted Oxborrow and his wife Jill of San Francisco. Ted was an athletic guy who wore a headband to secure his long hair. Jill was a petite blonde.

Their kids, a boy toddler and a girl a few years older, were well behaved and seemed to thoroughly enjoy the outer islands. The little boy never tired of running the native children ragged. In keeping with local custom, he went diaperless.

Whereas the little island boys were naked, the little girls always wore grass skirts.

Although Yapese women of all ages were topless, showing any skin between the waist and knee was strictly forbidden. As the saying goes, pornography is a matter of geography.

There was a flashy Melanesian woman aboard the ship who was said to be prostitute entertaining the crew.

She went ashore at one island wearing a miniskirt, thereby horrifying the local women. I didn't witness it but I was told the women grabbed her, pulled her into a house and redressed her, tossing her out with a skirt of the prescribed length and no top.

I don't believe she ever went ashore again.

In his book, *America's Paradise Lost,* Willard Price tells of a former district administrator in Yap who decided the women must cover their breasts. He bought and distributed white T-shirts to solve the problem.

The women wore them, but when they couldn't nurse their babies, they cut two holes in front, nicely framing the problem. The administrator gave up.

With the *Ran Annim* bobbing at anchor in the Lamotrek lagoon during the chiefs' conference, I tried sleeping ashore the first night. Once was enough.

I was offered a spot on the floor of one of the houses. With only my thin beach towel separating me from a sand-encrusted mat of woven palm fronds, it not only was uncomfortable but the mosquitoes drove me mad. Although I knew they didn't carry any diseases, sleeping was impossible.

I tried moving into what was called the dispensary – a hut with virtually nothing in it, but that wasn't much of an improvement. Of course none of the buildings had doors or windows. The thin mattress on the ship suddenly seemed very inviting, especially because the mosquitoes remained ashore.

At the feast following the conference, the chiefs and other dignitaries sat cross-legged facing each other across a three-foot wide row of mats stacked with food, about 20 men on each side. The women, who had spent close to 24 hours preparing the feast, sat with their children off on the side. Presumably they got a chance to eat at some point.

After the feast, 16 girls aged from about six to 16 lined up to provide the entertainment. Wearing ceremonial headbands and skirts, they swayed gently and moved their hands gracefully while singing. There was no musical accompaniment. It was strictly voices and it was enchanting.

Before the ship got to Lamotrek, the two Swedish medical students, both young men, got off at one of the stops to experience island life for a week or so.

Normally the ship would call at each island only once on a field trip. But because of the conference, it picked up chiefs at each island, took them to Lamotrek, then dropped them off on the way back.

When the Swedes returned to the ship, they were covered all over with little splotches of Mercurochrome to treat insect bites and scratches. They had also used antibiotics, keeping in mind that a tiny scratch in the tropics can develop into a nasty infection.

They weren't the only ones developing infections from scratches. I had some. Even the doctor had some. Many bruises were acquired from banging one's shins on the rusty metal stairs aboard the ship.

The voyage had been scheduled to last two weeks. After that mark passed, the number one topic of conversation each day was how soon we might be back in Colonia. As it turned out, it was 8:45 a.m. on Day 20.

The first thing I did ashore was book a seat on a plane leaving for Guam several hours later. Next, I ran to a snack bar and had two helpings of ice cream, then picked up the few things I had left at the hotel.

The flight to Guam lasted two and a half hours. Airline food never tasted so good.

Once in Guam, I immediately bought a round trip ticket to Saipan, boarded another plane and was there by evening.

The finale

Saipan was the cleanest and most modern of all the district centers. Everything was spread out with buildings sometimes miles apart.

The next morning, I went to a car rental office and arranged for a car so I could see the sights. Before I could start the engine, two guys I had met on the plane from Guam, California hippies, showed up. They were going to do the same thing, so I cancelled my car and went with them.

We visited an area called Garapan first to see a red Japanese locomotive and a prison, then drove to the north coast to look at the last Japanese command post.

Back in Guam for most of two days, I tracked down Bruce, one of the professors from the ship, and spent time with him, his wife and two children. He loaned me one of his cars to look for World War Two tanks that had been left on a battlefield.

Bruce was very generous. The Swedish medical students had shown up before me and borrowed the car. I had to wait until they returned it.

Flying home, I made an overnight stop in Honolulu to break the journey and lessen the jetlag. One thing I did was go to the Queen's Hospital emergency room to have the sores on my shins looked at. The only remarkable thing about that was the fact that the ER bill was only $16, not counting an antibiotic and ointment.

The Micronesian governments have changed considerably in the 40 years since I was there.
The Trust Territory no longer exists.
The Northern Marianas are now a U.S. Commonwealth.
The rest of the islands are independent, divided into three groups: the Marshall Islands, Palau and the Federated

States of Micronesia (FSM).

Making up the FSM are Yap, Ponape, Truk and Kusaie – all geographically part of the Caroline Islands. Yap is still called Yap. But the other groups are now known as Pohnpei, Chuuk and Kosrae. Kosrae used to be included in the Ponape district.

Not only was Truk changed to Chuuk, but the district center, Moen, was renamed Weno.

South Pacific

Tahiti & the golden letter

I made it to Tahiti and the rest of the South Pacific a year and a half later, flying out of Los Angeles in the summer of 1972.

A few weeks before leaving, I sent a letter to Pan Am asking if we could work out a deal whereby I could be paid for mentioning the airline in my articles.

Although purists might consider such a thing to be questionable if not outrageous, I didn't feel there would be anything unethical about it as long as I was honest. I had no idea what other travel writers did regarding that sort of thing. I didn't even know any travel writers.

A short time after I sent the letter, I got a call from the Pan Am public relations office asking for details about my freelance work. I rattled off which papers I wrote for and laid out my itinerary, never expecting anything to come of it.

I was surprised when a letter from Pan Am arrived the very day I was scheduled to leave. It said:

> This letter, when signed by you, will constitute an agreement between you and Pan American World Airways, Inc. (Pan Am), for a research and writing assignment as set forth below:
>
> You will write a series of five feature-length stories on Australia, New Zealand, Fiji, Samoa, Noumea and Tahiti. These stories will feature the following facets of Pan Am's operation: tours and flight services.
>
> Stories will appear in the Los Angeles Times, Chicago Tribune, Boston Globe, San Francisco Examiner and the Toronto Star during

1972. One article will appear in each of the above named newspapers, and each article will be different.

All travel and other expenses in connection with this assignment will be paid by you.

Pan American will be accorded exclusive airline mention throughout the articles.

Upon completion of the above and upon receipt of the clippings demonstrating the satisfactory fulfillment thereof, Pan Am agrees to pay you the sum of $1,225.

Very truly yours,
A. Lutz
Sr. Director Public Relations

I knew right away that fulfilling the agreement would be impossible because not every paper would print every story. Also, there was no way I'd write an article differently for each paper and I certainly had no intention of mentioning Pan Am's "tour and flight services." Nevertheless, I stuck the letter in my luggage and flew out of Los Angeles shortly after midnight on August 8 to begin exploring the South Pacific.

I arrived in the Tahitian capital, Papeete, at 5 a.m. A few hours later, I had a room at the Hotel Stuart, an older hotel overlooking the harbor at the west end of the business district. Although it was seedy, the place was loaded with atmosphere. A plaque in my fourth floor room noted that the French Impressionist Henri Matisse had stayed there in 1930.

For a daily rate of $7.20, I had a large room with a double bed, a private cold water bathroom and a dusty balcony with table and rocking chair.

The view was incredible. From the chair, I could watch the Super Rich come and go from luxurious sailboats bobbing at anchor along the quay, sailboats with home ports such as Seattle, San Francisco and Southampton. Forming a backdrop behind the rigging, 11 miles across the sea, was the jagged silhouette of Tahiti's sister island, Moorea.

Between the hotel and quay was a four lane street that looked as if it had been freshly blacktopped. There was a grassy tree-lined median equipped with an underground sprinkler system. Parking meters had recently been installed on the hotel side of the street. Traffic was a frantic mix of cars, brightly colored rickety buses, motor scooters and bicycles.

One of the anachronisms of life in Papeete was the sight of an attractive Tahitian woman dressed in a wraparound dress called a *pareu* whizzing by on a scooter with her long black hair streaming from beneath a crash helmet.

Balconied wooden buildings with red tile roofs were gradually being replaced with plain boxy structures. New supermarkets were competing with the old Chinese-run general stores.

Papeete, with a population of 30,000, had a laundromat and a tropical fish shop. Television had arrived, along with a drive-in movie theater.

Despite all that, especially the presence of the parking meters, some travel writers were still describing Tahiti as "unspoiled." I couldn't have disagreed more. In fact, when I wrote my article, I chided other writers for "challenging Somerset Maugham with purple prose."

The despoiling of French Polynesia actually began in 1595 when four Spanish ships captained by Alvaro de Mendaña landed at Fatu Hiva in the Marquesas. By the time he and his crew left, bullets and syphilis had killed 200 islanders.

The destruction of Old Tahiti became complete 50 years ago, in 1961, when the Papeete airstrip was lengthened and commercial jets started landing. Before that, Tahiti had 1,500 annual visitors who had not arrived on cruise ships. Afterward, the total swelled to 8,000. Now that number is easily surpassed each month.

I spent the first day getting familiar with Papeete. On my second morning, I took a bus to the 200-room Hotel Tahara'a, owned by Pan Am's Intercontinental chain. It was six miles east of Papeete, perched on a promontory that towered above the black sand beach where Capt. Cook and other explorers had come ashore in the late 1700s.

Most of the other hotels were on the opposite side of Papeete, just beyond the airport, which was three miles from town.

I had to look over the Tahara'a because it was the newest and best hotel on the island. It was built terrace-style with the floors staggered like steps, giving each room a view of Moorea. When you got on the elevator, you went down to the rooms, not up.

I met with the manager, James Harrell, and showed him my letter from Pan Am, along with a sheet of paper on which I had photocopied headlines and bylines from half a dozen travel articles.

His reaction: "Why don't you stay here?"

He made it clear it wouldn't cost me anything. I'd never given any thought to trying to work out a deal on a room. But suddenly the letter had turned to gold.

The next morning, I checked out of the Hotel Stuart. When I told Mrs. Stuart, a portly Tahitian woman, that I was leaving because I had a free room at the Tahara'a, she said I could have stayed at her place for free too. I declined.

I moved into a plush room that normally cost $36 per day. Whatever atmosphere the hotel had on the outside disappeared when I entered the room. With the draperies closed, I could have been in a Holiday Inn in Philadelphia. But it did have a private bath with hot water.

One disadvantage of the Tahara'a, besides being a bit far from Papeete, was that there was no easy access to the beach because the hotel was high above the water. Virtually every other tourist hotel was just a few steps from the surf.

Whenever possible, I ate breakfast at the hotel – a lavish outdoor buffet. I had to pay for it: $3.50. But it was worth it.

I dutifully visited half a dozen other hotels, inspecting rooms and noting the prices. I always thought that was the worst part of being a travel writer. In the article I later wrote, I mentioned six hotels including the Tahara'a and the Stuart, describing the Tahara'a as "luxurious" and the Stuart as "grubby."

I could hardly wait to see Papeete's most well-known man-made attraction, Quinn's Bar, a watering hole mentioned occasionally in South Seas literature.

It was a raucous place midway along the waterfront. There were two wide entrances. Between them, just inside the doors, was a platform where a small band played. A few steps further was the bar. Tahitians were often dancing.

I was surprised to find that Quinn's had a unisex restroom. But that was fitting in a way because some of the patrons were husky transvestites dressed in garish costumes.

Fortunately I had arrived in Tahiti just in time to experience Quinn's. The following year, the legendary bar was torn down to make way for a shopping center.

It was clear from the start that Tahitians were still easy-going people who believed human beings were put on Earth to have a good time.

Tahitian women used flowers to indicate their availability. A flower over the left ear meant they were spoken for. On the right, it signified they not only were single but looking. A flower placed anywhere else in the hair meant that, for whatever reason, they were not interested.

Riding the buses provided a good insight into Tahitian attitudes. A bus was called *le truck,* and with good reason. Each was a homemade vehicle built on a truck chassis. They headed out from the central market to coastal villages with their destination painted on the side. The standard fare was 25¢. Passengers hopped aboard from the rear and sat on benches along the sides facing each other. Bulky packages and animals rode on top.

To satisfy the Tahitian love for music, each driver played audio cassettes. The bus never moved until everyone was seated and service was extra slow before mealtimes because the buses stopped at shops along the way to let passengers buy fresh baguettes and other last-minute items. No one ever seemed to be in a hurry.

Eating French bread was just one of the Gallic habits the Tahitians cheerfully adopted since the French formally took control of their islands in the late 1800s. They also greeted friends and relatives by kissing them on both cheeks, something they did with great gusto.

Decorated T-shirts were popular. Most simply said "Tahiti" or featured the names of other islands or commercial products such as local breweries. However, I spotted a teenage girl wearing one labeled, "Chicago Park District."

The best free entertainment in Papeete was the docking of a cruise ship. They came in twice a month. Just before a ship arrived, more than a dozen souvenir stands would spring up along the wharf. A troupe of dancers was usually on hand to greet the disembarking tourists. The grass-skirted dancers did a condensed version of a hotel floorshow.

Circling Tahiti by thumb

The road that encircles Tahiti is 114 km or 71 miles long. That's not counting Tahiti-Iti (Little Tahiti), a large peninsula jutting off the back side of the island. On a map, the two pieces of land resemble a distorted number 8, with the island much larger than the appendage.

I happened to be in Tahiti on the Feast of the Assumption, a big holiday during which everything was closed. That seemed to be a good time to travel around the island, which I decided to do by hitchhiking.

Hitching turned out to be very good. After only 10 minutes, I got a lift from a man in an old red Volkswagen who took me about five km.

After another 10 minutes or so, I traveled about 50 km with a middle-aged Tahitian woman who was going to what apparently was her country home on Tahiti-Iti. The scenery along the road was fantastic. On the side opposite the sea was a dense green rain forest climbing to mountain peaks that rose as high as 7,000 feet.

After arriving at the woman's home, we relaxed for a while with a glass of wine. Then she drove me back to the main road so I could catch another ride. Meeting the locals is the greatest benefit of hitchhiking.

My next lift took me to the Gauguin Museum, located almost directly across the island from Papeete. It was built where the French Impressionist Paul Gauguin had lived between 1896 and 1901. I enjoyed the museum, which featured displays tracing his life on Tahiti. There were no original paintings of course.

What was probably the last piece of Gauguin artwork in Tahiti was discovered by Somerset Maugham when he visited the island in 1917 to research his fictional account of the artist's life, *The Moon and Sixpence.*

Maugham learned that Gauguin had painted over glass panes in the door of a small house where he had stayed while recovering from an illness.

There originally had been three paintings. Children had scratched two of them off the glass. The third, which was spread over six panes, was only slightly damaged. It showed the biblical Eve holding an apple.

The man who owned the house told Maugham he could have the painting as long as he replaced the door. Maugham immediately arranged for a replacement and had the door removed. After the painting was separated from the rest of the door, he had it crated in Papeete and shipped to his home in France.

In his book, *Somerset Maugham*, Ted Morgan writes: "When Maugham sold his art collection at Sotheby's in 1962, the Gauguin door sold for $37,400."

The most curious item at the Gauguin Museum was a stone tiki in the garden that Tahitians were said to fear. According to Tahitian lore, anyone who moves a tiki risks incurring a curse, and that one had been brought from another island. There may have been something to the curse. I heard from more than one source that several people who handled the tiki died within weeks.

Leaving the museum, I got a final lift from an Englishman who took me all the way back to Papeete.

The 'dangerous islands'

I had hoped to travel by ship to the distant Marquesas, where Gauguin had also lived and was buried, but that didn't work out, so I set my sights on Rangiroa, an atoll in the Tuamotu Archipelago. The Marquesas are 500 miles northeast of Tahiti. Rangiroa is in the same direction, 200 miles away.

Emboldened by my success in getting a free hotel room, I visited the tourist office, met with the director, Jacques Briquet, and got a free plane ticket to Rangiroa. The tourist office split the cost with the airline, UTA.

Unlike mountainous Tahiti, the Tuamotus are low and flat, so low that navigators long ago nicknamed them the "dangerous islands" because many ships had run aground.

Rangiroa, the largest atoll in the group, is a string of islands surrounding a lagoon measuring 42 by 14 miles. The main island is a strip of white sand and palm trees about seven miles long.

Getting there took one hour on a Fokker F-25 prop plane. The only other outsiders traveling to the island were a French couple named Robin and Serge. After the crowd cleared at the air strip, the three of us traveled by bus to the only town on the island, Avatoru.

The houses were modern. Everyone who could afford it replaced his thatched roof with corrugated metal and filled his window frames with glass shutters. Few homes, however, had doors – just long strips of colored plastic to keep the flies out. The islanders dressed in casual clothing.

There was no hotel. The first one was under construction and scheduled to open soon. Visitors were put up in private homes at a cost of less than $10 per person per day. For that, they got a bed, a lukewarm rainwater shower that didn't always work because of a water shortage and three meals a day, usually fish and eggs.

Robin and Serge took a room in one of the homes. I had brought a pup tent with me, new and bright blue, and I decided to use it. I set it up in a small clearing outside the town, making sure there were no coconuts directly above me. The same soft breezes that rustle the fronds can also loosen the nuts, causing them to streak to the ground like cannon balls.

I felt foolish camping out and the islanders probably thought I was crazy. I should at least have asked permission. On a Pacific island, every inch of land, every palm tree and every coconut is owned by someone and I was undoubtedly trespassing. But no one complained.

Sleeping in the tent was less than comfortable, especially since I had left my air mattress in Tahiti to cut down on weight. (I never used the tent again. After lugging it across the Pacific, I sold it in a pawn shop in Sydney.)

I had arrived on a Wednesday and was leaving on Saturday, giving me two full days on Rangiroa. I spent some of the time alone and some with Robin and Serge. On Thursday afternoon, I joined them in traveling to the next island by pickup truck and boat.

With no organized activities, exploring the island was about the only thing there was to do. On the lagoon side, a sandy beach slipped into the lagoon where I swam through crystal clear waters watching colorful fish swim by.

At one point, I almost stepped on a ray that was half buried in the sand, something they tend to do. It scared the hell out of both me and the ray, which took off like a shot. It happened so fast I couldn't tell whether it was a harmless manta ray or a sting ray, which has a barb at the end of the tail that could have sliced my foot open.

On the ocean side was a rugged reef that was tougher than concrete. At low tide, I walked among the tidal pools as hermit crabs scattered for cover. The roaring surf broke along the edge of the reef, covering me with a salty mist.

The only other diversions were watching boys fishing off the village wharf or picking up a cool bottle of beer or strawberry soda at the village store, which was little more than a kiosk with an attractive *pareu*-clad young woman behind the counter.

There was no restaurant on the island, but I didn't have to partake of the fish and eggs served in the homes. I had brought some canned goods with me and bought more at the store. My meals consisted of things such as canned tuna and beans accompanied by potato chips and soda from the store.

I wrote a story about Rangiroa that got good play, including the front page of the *LA Times* travel section. The airline and the tourist office hadn't wasted the plane ticket.

Tahiti's sister island

Back in Papeete, I traveled by boat to nearby Moorea. The ride took 90 minutes. When heading over in the morning, the sea is calm, but it's usually rough for the late afternoon return. It was also possible to fly there in a matter of minutes.

With a coastline of 59 km or 37 miles, Moorea is roughly half the size of the main part of Tahiti. There were no sizable towns, but the island boasted eight major hotels, including Club Med, which was fairly new at the time. Most of the hotels were self-contained resorts featuring Polynesian-style over-the-water thatched roof bungalows, some with kitchenettes.

There were plenty of activities for guests. Hotels provided bicycles, outrigger canoes and snorkeling gear free of charge. Cars, scooters and sailboats were available for rental. Some hotels staged weekly Tahitian dance shows.

Bali Ha'i is calling

In order to touch all the bases for my articles, I also wanted to visit the Leeward Islands, located between 80 and 200 miles northwest of Tahiti. They include Raiatea, Huahine and Bora Bora.

I tracked down two ships that were sailing to the Leewards almost immediately, but one was taking oil, not passengers, and the other was fully booked. So I talked with Monsieur Briquet at the tourist office again and wound up with a plane ticket on Air Polynesie.

I flew first to Bora Bora, regarded as one of the most beautiful islands in the Pacific.

It's said that James Michener had Bora Bora in mind when he wrote of Bali Ha'i in his novel, *Tales of the South Pacific,* which Richard Rodgers and Oscar Hammerstein later turned into the award-winning musical *South Pacific.* That may be true. But the source of the name was a village on a small island in the Solomons that Michener came across while serving as a U.S. naval officer during World War Two.

In his book *Return to Paradise,* he writes, "We stumbled into a filthy, unpleasant village bearing one of the loveliest names I've ever heard: Bali-ha'i. From my pocket I drew a scrap of paper, soggy with sweat, and thought, 'I'll take a note of that name. It has a musical quality.' Years later, Rodgers and Hammerstein were to think the same."

From an arriving plane, the most impressive sight was the twin mountain peaks in the center of Bora Bora which towered more than 2,000 feet, creating a striking profile from any angle. A reef dotted with tiny islets surrounded the island, sheltering a shallow lagoon. The airstrip was on one of the islets. Passengers were ferried to the island by a small boat.

My only complaint about Bora Bora was that the number one hotel, the Bora Bora, cost more than the best hotels on Tahiti but wasn't as good. But I had arranged for a free room, so it didn't matter.

My plane ticket included a hop to a small island called Maupiti, located about 30 miles away, so I went. Maupiti was just as beautiful as Bora Bora but totally undeveloped when it came to tourism. The only other people aboard the small plane were the pilot and a ticket agent.

Once again, the airstrip was on the reef and we traveled ashore by boat. We were there for four hours. I walked around what appeared to be the only village. There were a few new cement houses, and some shacks too. Virtually every house had a red corrugated metal roof. The people were very friendly. Nearly everyone waved.

The pilot and I had lunch at the only restaurant in the village – two kinds of fish plus fruit, bread and coffee. Then we flew back to Bora Bora.

I was only there for one overnight, long enough to look around and inspect the other two hotels. In the morning, I spotted a ship coming in and went to see where it was headed. I was in luck. It was sailing for Raiatea in mid-afternoon. Since I wanted to see Raiatea and preferred to go by surface, I bought a ticket for $1.98.

The three-hour trip was pleasant. There were scarcely more than a dozen passengers.

It was dark when we arrived at Raiatea. I had no trouble hitching a ride to the Bali Ha'i hotel, where I was once again successful in getting a free room. The manager, Tim Drost, even bought me dinner. Unlike some of the other hotels I'd seen, the Bali Ha'i was very nice.

The next morning, I grabbed one of the hotel's bikes and spent three hours pedaling around. The village, called Uturoa, was several blocks long. There were two streets paralleling the waterfront with a market in the middle.

I had to see the third principal island, Huahine, which was only 30 miles away, but none of the boat or plane schedules worked for me. I mentioned that to Mr. Drost and he suggested chartering a plane. That was a radical idea for someone who begged for free hotel rooms, but I couldn't write a story about the Leewards without visiting Huahine.

I agreed to pay for a charter. Drost made a phone call and a short while later I was on my way to the airport in the hotel minibus which was heading there to pick up passengers.

The pilot was a rotund Tahitian in his late 40s with long white hair and the unlikely name of Charley Higgins. Charley and I squeezed into his Piper Cub and were over Huahine buzzing the village in no time. It was a real roller coaster ride.

Drost had phoned the manager of a hotel that was under construction and he picked us up at the airport. The dive bombing was Charley's way of alerting him to our arrival.

The manager gave us a ride into town, which was essentially one street measuring four blocks long. Charley and I split up as I looked over the area as well as the hotels. Then it was back to the airport and Raiatea. From takeoff to touchdown, we had been gone for two hours and 15 minutes. The tab for the charter was $32.50.

The next day I flew back to Papeete.

The only problem I had in Tahiti occurred when I made my final trip to the airport to leave for American Samoa.

I went on the hotel bus. When we got to the airport, my suitcase was nowhere to be seen. The driver apparently had left it sitting in front of the hotel. I insisted he phone the hotel and have it sent out. He did phone, then reported that nothing could be done – a case of South Pacific mentality.

I tried to phone the hotel myself but couldn't get through, so I asked a Pan Am clerk to try. The receptionist at the hotel told him he'd put the suitcase in a taxi. It arrived a short time later. I got stuck paying the driver $7 for the delivery. Despite the delay, I made my flight.

I had spent nearly three weeks in French Polynesia using the Tahara'a as a base. I would have moved on a lot sooner if the room hadn't been free.

I wrote four stories, covering Tahiti, Moorea, Rangiroa and the Leeward Islands. I later squeezed out a fifth article by wrapping up everything in a piece called "South Pacific: Once Over Lightly."

I had to write as much as possible to make any money. The standard payment for an article in major Sunday papers was $35, plus $15 for each photograph. The *LA Times* paid $75 when I was lucky enough to make the front page of the travel section with photo.

The Tahara'a went out of business a number of years ago and the building has been vacant. The creaky old Hotel Stuart was torn down.

The Samoas: divided by history

There are two Samoas, and they're very different.

American Samoa is an unincorporated territory of the United States under the jurisdiction of the Department of the Interior. Just plain Samoa, formerly known as Western Samoa, is independent.

The two Samoas have been separated since 1899 when Germany and the United States drew an imaginary line though the islands and set up individual administrations. Of course no one consulted the Samoans.

New Zealand evicted Germany in 1914 and governed until Western Samoa achieved independence in 1962. In 1997, the islanders dropped the word Western.

This is how I began my article about Western Samoa:

> You may already know that Samoa is divided into two parts. This is its better half.

I went on to explain that unlike American Samoa and other major islands, Western Samoa had held fast to its ancient culture. Nowhere else in the South Pacific, I wrote, could you find a place that fit the classic image of the old South Seas as well.

American Samoa, on the other hand, wasn't nearly as interesting because it was, to put it simply, Americanized. Forget grass skirts. The teenagers were wearing tee shirts and sawed-off blue jeans.

I flew directly from Papeete to Pago Pago, the capital of American Samoa, located on the main island of Tutuila. It was a three hour flight on a Pan Am 707. There was a time change. Watches were set back one hour.

A week before leaving Tahiti, I had sent a letter to the best hotel, the Americana (formerly the Intercontinental), requesting a free room. I got one. After arriving, I discovered there were only two hotels anyway. The Americana was in the heart of tiny Pago Pago, on the edge of the harbor. The other hotel was seven miles out.

It was difficult to write about American Samoa because frankly it wasn't very exciting. Pago Pago was a small one-street town hugging a narrow strip of land between the mountains and the harbor. Aside from a few modern buildings, the offices and stores fronting the village green were old wooden structures, many painted white.

In order to add interest to my article, I worked in a mention of Sadie Thompson, the good-time girl who corrupted the incorruptible Reverend Davidson in Somerset Maugham's celebrated short story "Rain."

Although Maugham's plot was fictional, researchers believe his characters were based on real people who sailed on the ship that took him to Pago Pago in 1916. In fact, the list of passengers aboard the steamer *Sonoma* at that time included a "Miss Thompson."

Sadie wouldn't have had trouble finding her way around. The boarding house where she was believed to have stayed had become Max Haleck's One Stop Market, a store that stocked such exotic items as instant breakfast mixes and frozen pizzas. She would have been pleased to learn that the main hotel had named its meeting hall Sadie's Place.

When it rained, as it often did, Sadie would no longer have to sit in her room and sing along with her Victrola. She could watch TV. The program schedule included shows such as *Bonanza, Mission Impossible, Star Trek* and, most popular of all, *The Fugitive*.

Even though I wasn't going out of my way to mention Pan Am, I tried to slip in the airline as a test of my creative abilities, and I came up with an idea that worked. I wrote that if a modern day Sadie caused a scandal and the governor saw fit to deport her to Hawaii, some 2,300 miles to the northeast, he wouldn't have to wait a week for a ship – he could hustle her aboard a Pan Am jet.

Pago Pago seemed almost as isolated as when Sadie was in town. There was no such thing as a daily newspaper. The only source of fresh news was a UPI teletype in the lobby of the Americana. The TV station broadcast the network news from ABC, but the programs were exactly one week late. In the days before satellites, tapes of the newscasts were flown in from Los Angeles.

It was possible to get a bird's eye view of Pago Pago by riding the aerial tram that soared across the harbor. The mile-long tramway was built to take engineers to the TV transmitter perched atop the 1,600 foot Rainmaker Mountain. It ran almost directly above the tuna processing factory, the major business in American Samoa.

I always looked for things to see and do that were part of normal life rather than something planned for tourists. Since the tourist industry was seriously underdeveloped in American Samoa, that was easy.

One thing I did was ride the minibuses that traveled to

each end of the 18-mile-long island. The eastern road was shorter and more scenic, threading its way past small bays with white sand beaches and pyramid-shaped rocks that poked through the breaking surf.

For a bit of adventure, I booked passage on a 60-foot ship called the *Manusina* that traveled around the island once each week delivering supplies to villages not served by roads.

There were seven Americans aboard besides me and a few Samoans. The ship started out loaded down with packages for five villages. Since there were no docks, villagers paddled out to the ship in their boats.

Rounding the west end of the island, the seas became heavy. Everyone got soaked as the ship pitched and plunged through swells running at least five feet high. Despite the rough waters, the trip didn't last any longer than the usual five hours. And the ticket was a bargain at $2.

Although scattered patches of rain had started pelting the island, I reluctantly bought a ticket for another sailing. A 140-foot ship known as the *Talistiga* was scheduled to leave at midnight for the Manu'a Islands, some 80 miles away. The Manu'a group was where Margaret Mead lived while researching her classic book *Coming of Age in Samoa*.

The rain continued all evening. Around 11 p.m., I decided the weather was just too lousy for me to get on the ship, so I went to sleep at the hotel. In the morning, I learned the ship hadn't left anyway. The sailing had been postponed until noon. Since the weather still looked ominous, I got a refund on my $5 ticket and forgot about Manu'a.

Maugham sure got it right when he titled his story "Rain."

After a week in American Samoa, I flew to the other Samoa, 80 miles away. The principal island, Upolu, is roughly 45 miles long from east to west and 15 miles wide. The capital, Apia, sits midway along the north coast.

The 20-mile ride from the airport to Apia was a pleasant introduction. The road followed a palm-fringed shoreline, crossing over little streams where children swam while their mothers did the family wash. We passed an almost continuous string of villages, each dominated by a cathedral-like church. I counted about three churches to the mile.

The people were still building open-sided thatch-roofed houses called *fales* and eating mainly fish, coconuts, breadfruit and bananas. The basic attire for men, women and children was the wraparound *lava-lava*.

Apia's population was around 28,000. Several large trading company buildings and a white clock tower lined the waterfront, giving the town a colonial atmosphere.

I headed straight for the top hotel on the island, Aggie Grey's. The legendary Aggie, who had a British father and a Samoan mother, got into the hotel business after World War Two, bankrolling it with money she had earned from selling hamburgers to U.S. servicemen.

It's generally believed that James Michener's character Bloody Mary, featured in *Tales of the South Pacific,* was based on Aggie. However, the two women seemed to have nothing in common other than being entrepreneurs. While Aggie Grey was a soft-spoken matronly woman with an almost regal air, the fictional Bloody Mary was a short, sassy Tonkinese whose teeth were stained black from chewing betel nut.

The Tonkinese came from the northernmost part of Vietnam, known as Tonkin when the country was a French colony. Before World War Two, French planters shipped many of them to the Pacific to work on their plantations.

Michener himself, in his 1992 memoir, *The World is My Home*, put an end to the Bloody Mary debate by flatly stating that she was a Tonkinese woman "about thirty-five, roundish in shape" he had met on the island of Espiritu Santo in the New Hebrides (now Vanuatu). "I never knew her real name," he wrote, "but she had come to be known as Bloody Mary, and that is how I still recall her"

It was Sunday when I arrived and there was no one in

the office with whom I could discuss a free room, so I registered and kept my fingers crossed.

Despite having more than 100 rooms, Aggie's managed to maintain a personal touch. In addition to the usual amenities such as a swimming pool and air conditioning, the rooms were equipped with irons and ironing boards. When Aggie was just beginning, guests often asked if they could borrow an iron, so she eventually put one in each room. Then along came permanent press and the irons were rarely used. But they were a nice touch anyway.

The next day, I introduced myself to the manager, Aggie's son Alan. He agreed to let me have a room for nothing. And that wasn't all. He explained that the daily rates ($18 single and $32 double) included meals, so I could eat for free too.

Mr. Grey was very accommodating when it came to helping me explore Western Samoa. He lined up a tour of Upolu for the next day and arranged a free plane ticket to the neighboring island of Savaii for the following day.

For the island tour, a pleasant woman named Anna, who ran the travel desk, spent five hours driving me to sights along the opposite coast. Traveling directly south across the island, we drove through rugged mountains rising as high as 2,000 feet. At the summit, called Le Mafa Pass, huge ferns formed a canopy over the road. We stopped briefly at a waterfall, then it was on to the gorgeous beach at Lefaga, where the 1953 movie *Return to Paradise,* starring Gary Cooper, was filmed. (On rare occasions, it turns up on Turner Classic Movies.) After enjoying box lunches on the beach provided by the hotel, we returned to Apia.

Meals were served boarding house style at Aggie's with guests seated haphazardly and everyone eating the same food. After the initial shock of dining with strangers, most guests grew to like the idea.

My dining partners often included Jody Hart and Virginia Adams, two longtime, slightly middle-aged friends who were traveling the Pacific together. Jody, a blonde, was from New York City and Virginia, a brunette with an Auntie Mame personality, was a New Jersey native living in Los Angeles.

Jody claimed to be a travel writer doing stories about the Pacific for American Airlines. Unlike me, however, she had no credentials. After seeing Mr. Grey, she wound up with a free plane ticket to Savaii but no freebies at the hotel.

Jody and I flew to Savaii on an Air Samoa eight-passenger propeller plane. It was a quick trip since the islands were only 10 miles apart. At 660 square miles, Savaii was one of the largest islands in the Pacific. It was also one of the most undeveloped when it came to tourism.

A minibus took us to the large two-story wood frame home of the airline's agent, Tui Va'ai. We asked about hiring a car and were told that one of Mr. Va'ai's men would drive us around in a truck for a fee of $12.20.

Off we went for the next three hours, driving along beautiful white sand beaches to the far end of the island to see the picturesque village of Falealupo, which looked out across the sea from the edge of a rain forest.

Falealupo was heavily damaged in a typhoon in 1991 and the traditional *fales* were replaced by modern homes.

After a box lunch back at the house, Jody and I tried hitchhiking. We were unsuccessful due to a severe lack of traffic. Since we hadn't seen as much as we wanted, we decided to stay overnight. There were no hotels. The only choice was Mr. Va'ai's house, which was sometimes used to bunk tourists. Although it was a private home, it had six bedrooms on the second floor because 10 children had once lived there at the same time.

We hired the truck and driver again the next day, this time for $20, and traveled entirely around the island, a distance of about 150 miles on unpaved roads. The scenery was incredible, ranging from classic tropical beaches to towering mountains in the interior. On the north coast, we passed through a thick banyan forest where beams of sunlight streaked to the ground like spotlights. The range of plant life was impressive – hibiscus, frangipani, taro, bananas, cocoa, kapok, breadfruit – a true Garden of Eden.

On the east coast were large lava fields. Some of the villages we passed were built on lava, some were in grassy areas and others on sand.

By late afternoon, Jody and I had paid $7.65 each for our overnight stay, including meals, and flew back to Upolu, arriving at Aggie's just in time to see a Samoan dance performance, known as a *fia fia*.

Unlike American Samoa but similar to Tahiti, there was plenty of nightlife. Apia had 16 nightclubs. Among the most popular was a spot called the Poly-Eur-Asian Club, which usually had live music on weekends.

The best-known attraction in Samoa was the home of Robert Louis Stevenson, the Scottish-born author who wrote such classics as *Treasure Island, Kidnapped* and *The Strange Case of Dr. Jekyll and Mr. Hyde.*

Stevenson had been in frail health his entire life, suffering from a chronic lung ailment believed to be tuberculosis. After extensive travel in the Pacific, he felt best in Samoa despite the hot, steamy climate, so he built a house – actually more of an estate – which he called Vailima. He lived there for the last four years of his life before being felled by a stroke in 1894 at the age of only 44.

Stevenson was greatly revered by the Samoans, who called him *Tusitala,* or Teller of Tales. They buried him at the summit of a mountain overlooking his home. Getting to the tomb is said to be an arduous climb which is especially difficult after it rains. I did not attempt it.

The simple white tomb bears a famous epitaph composed by Stevenson himself:

> Under the wide and starry sky,
> Dig the grave and let me lie.
> Glad did I live and gladly die,
> And I laid me down with a will.
>
> This be the verse you grave for me:
> Here he lies where he longed to be;
> Home is the sailor, home from the sea,
> And the hunter home from the hill.

Stevenson's house has changed hands many times. When I was there, it was off limits to visitors because the head of state lived there. It's still the official residence of the head of state but in recent years the carefully restored home has been open to the public as a museum.

One thing I wanted to do before leaving Samoa was visit a tiny island named Manono, located three and a half miles off the west end of Upolu. After spending an hour and 15 minutes on a bus getting to the end of the island, I caught a boat for the 20 minute ride across the shallow lagoon, which was pale green in color.

In the middle of the lagoon was one tiny island with five palm trees on it, looking as if it had escaped from a desert isle cartoon.

There were some modern houses and some shacks on the island but most homes were *fales,* giving Manono an outer island feeling. There was no electricity, no vehicles either, not even a road – just a path connecting the villages, each of which had its own boat parked on the beach.

I walked for half an hour until it started to rain. A woman invited me into her *fale* to keep dry. It was a typical one room house with a thatched roof and woven mats on the sides that could be raised or lowered depending on the weather or time of day. We talked for nearly an hour, asking questions of each other. The woman spoke English well, as did most Samoans. She introduced me to her attractive teenaged daughter, Vienna.

As I started to leave, the woman expressed surprise, saying she was fixing a meal for me. However, she said it wouldn't be ready for an hour. I told her that was fine because I wanted to finish walking around the island. She sent two little boys with me as companions, probably to make sure I came back.

Manono measured a bit more than one square mile, meaning the circumference was probably three miles.

The villages thinned out on the back side. Walking slowly, we made it back in an hour and a half. Despite overcast skies, it was a pleasant walk.

The meal turned out to be breadfruit chips, a soup of fish and cabbage plus homemade cocoa. It was very good.

Cocoa beans grow inside purple pods measuring seven or eight inches long. I watched as the woman ground roasted beans into a powder, then mixed it with sugar and boiling water.

After dinner, I was invited to stay overnight, but I had to decline because I was catching a plane in the morning.

Vienna walked me to the pier. I grew concerned when several people told us I had missed the regular boat and there wouldn't be another. But we soon learned that an unscheduled boat was due. The boat that turned up had been chartered for a beach party and I had no trouble getting a lift back to Upolu.

My luck held out a while longer. Two men on the boat gave me a ride all the way to Apia in their pickup truck. If it hadn't been for them, I might have missed my flight.

Feasting in the last Polynesian kingdom

I hadn't planned to visit Tonga. I added the island kingdom to my itinerary when I learned it cost only a few dollars more to stop off there on my way to Fiji.

Arriving about a week before a royal feast was scheduled, I decided to hang around and see what it was like.

The feast was a birthday celebration for the prime minister's infant grandson, staged on the lawn in front of King Taufa'ahau Tupou IV's white frame, Victorian-style palace in the center of Nuku'alofa, the capital.

An estimated 1,000 people attended, half of them invited guests and the rest onlookers. As a journalist, I managed to get an invitation from the tourist office.

The guests gathered under tarpaulins erected to provide shade. They sat on the ground facing each other across low tables piled high with roasted pig, chicken, crab, taro, watermelon and a variety of other fruits, eating with their hands. Waiters and waitresses served bottles of orange soda.

There were speeches. A brass band played and a dozen different dance groups took turns performing. The whole affair lasted three hours. No one left hungry.

I lost one day flying to Tonga, which brushes up against the west side of the International Dateline. By coincidence, Jody and Virginia were on the same flight. The first thing we did was hop into a taxi for the 14-mile drive into Nuku'alofa, where we checked into the Dateline Hotel. The best I could do was a 50% discount. Then Jody and I went to the tourist office to line up a series of tours.

Tonga, the last kingdom in Polynesia, seemed a bit run down compared with other island groups. The rigidly stratified population was composed of chiefs, nobles and commoners, most of whom seemed content with their place in life. The people appeared to be stockier than Tahitians and Samoans.

Tonga had never been under foreign rule. However, it did not escape foreign influence. Missionaries from the Wesleyan Methodist Church imbued the people with a zealous dedication to Christianity. As a result, it was against the law to perform any kind of work on Sunday, women swam fully clothed and a man could be arrested for appearing in public without a shirt.

Although Tonga includes 150 islands, three-fifths of the 88,000 inhabitants lived on the main island of Tongatapu.

Nuku'alofa was small by any standard. The central business district consisted of one street five blocks long, lined mostly with old wooden buildings. However, there was a new supermarket and a modern post office.

Taxi service was provided by colorful little three-wheeled motorbikes. Horse-drawn carts outnumbered cars.

A man from the government tourist office gave me and Jody a tour of the main sights using a car provided by one of the travel agencies. It was more interesting than I had expected. Braving a light rain, we traveled to the west end of the island to see the blowholes – hundreds of geysers that shot more than 30 feet into the air.

Another top attraction was the Ha'amonga trilithon – three huge blocks of coral that formed what looked like a giant doorway. It was built centuries ago, and may have been part of a residence.

Getting a quick look at everything that might interest tourists, we also checked out the sacred flying foxes hanging from trees in an outlying village and the terraced tombs where members of the royal family were buried.

Another essential stop was the spot where Captain Cook landed in 1773.

Like other tiny nations, Tonga did a good business selling large, sometimes gaudy postage stamps.

Tongan handicrafts were well regarded, especially the geometrically patterned tapa cloth made by flattening mulberry bark with a heavy mallet.

Fiji and the girls of Vanua Vatu

Compared with most other Pacific island nations, Fiji was a well-oiled tourist factory.

It had by far the greatest number of hotels, plus a wide range of well-organized tours and cruises. Duty-free shops in Suva and other major population centers offered bargains on watches, cameras and transistor radios.

Sometimes called the Crossroads of the Pacific, Fiji was home to a diverse population. The native Fijians, who are black-skinned Melanesians, were outnumbered by people from India who were brought in many years earlier to harvest sugar cane and wound up taking over most of the plantations and businesses. There also were large numbers of Europeans, Chinese, Samoans and other Pacific islanders.

Despite the massive assault on their culture, Fijians were still smiling and living in thatched huts called *bures* in rural areas.

Fiji became a British Crown Colony in 1874, a time when cannibalism was prevalent, and gained independence in 1970.

Upon arriving in the capital, Suva, on the main island of Viti Levu, I used the Pan Am letter and my travel writer credentials to convince the Fiji Visitors Bureau to set me up with a bunch of freebies. I was there for three weeks and got all but one hotel room and many meals free.

The visitors bureau flew me to two of the other major islands, Vanua Levu and Taveuni, to look over the sights. I saw nothing that appealed to me so I didn't write anything. There's no way I would have promoted any place simply because I got a free trip there.

One excursion that was definitely worth writing about – and I did – was a weeklong voyage on a ship that served as the principal means of transport to some of the outer islands.

The ship was the *Uluilakeba* – 112 feet long, six years old and a bit rusty for her age.

She steamed out of Suva three times each month to the Lau islands, 150 miles to the east, carrying passengers and cargo. She returned with passengers and copra.

The *Uluilakeba* was not to be confused with a cruise ship. She was more like those lumbering old steamers that Maugham wrote about.

She had space for 10 passengers in two four-berth cabins and one two-berth. Each cabin was sparsely furnished with a closet, a cold water wash basin and a medicine cabinet. Floor space measured about five by 10 feet. The bathroom, equipped with a lukewarm shower, was down the hall.

There was only one table in the tiny dining room. If the passengers numbered more than five, they'd have to eat in shifts. The meals – three each day plus morning and afternoon tea – were excellent, and the cheerful, white-coated steward added a touch of decorum by presenting each diner with a hand-written menu.

The *Uluilakeba* made alternate voyages to the north, central and southern Lau islands, a group scattered over a stretch of ocean measuring 150 miles north to south and 50 miles east to west. The ship didn't have enough cargo space to serve all the islands in one outing. I went on the central trip because that was the one that happened to be leaving.

Although I was told the ship was sometimes fully booked, there were only two other cabin passengers. One was a Fijian man returning to one of the islands. The other was a 40-something New Zealand bank clerk making his second voyage on the ship.

There also were about a dozen deck passengers who slept on cots at the back of the ship.

According to the steward, a number of individuals and families from Australia and New Zealand had spent more than one of their vacations on the ship. The most famous passenger was the actor Raymond Burr, who played Perry Mason on TV. He owned one of the northern islands.

We called at four islands including Lakeba, home of the prime minister and the most highly developed island in the group. Most of the homes there had metal roofs instead of the traditional thatched roofs seen on other islands.

Even on the outer islands, the Fijians wore regular clothes – no grass skirts or anything exotic.

Before we left Lakeba, a family got on with a homemade crate carrying three pigs and a rooster. The bird *cock-a-doodle-dood* all afternoon, adding a bit of local color.

As I had grown to expect, the amount of time spent at each island varied depending on the cargo. It was anywhere from several hours to a full day.

Since there were no docking facilities at any of the islands, those heading ashore rode in a small boat that was boarded by climbing down the side of the ship on an iron ladder. Once ashore, passengers could explore the village, go swimming and snorkeling in the lagoon or walk along the beach looking for sea shells.

There was plenty of time to talk with the natives, most of whom spoke English well. At every island, they seemed to ask the same questions:

"What is your name?"

"Where do you come from?"

"Are you married?"

The most enthusiastic reception we received was on a little island named Vanua Vatu. The New Zealander and I arrived on the beach just after dark to be greeted with handshakes from more than a dozen giggling young women. After everyone was introduced, two of them grabbed us by the hands and led us into the village.

I couldn't imagine what they were up to. We wound up in one of the huts, sitting cross-legged around a hissing gas lantern. After we met a few more people, the girls borrowed a pen and a piece of paper from my companion, wrote down their names and addresses, then returned the paper, saying, "When you get back home, could you please send us some bobby pins?"

I must confess I did not send any bobby pins to the girls of Vanua Vatu. I neglected to copy their address.

There were some tense moments as the boat left Vanua Vatu in the pitch dark, heavily loaded with people, luggage and sacks of copra. It was low tide and there was no gap in the reef. While traveling over it, we crunched to a stop several times and got swamped by the breaking waves. Each time, a couple of men jumped over the side and shoved the boat forward – certainly more exciting than the Blue Lagoon Cruise back in Suva.

The voyage should have cost $77 but I sailed for free. The shipping company gave me a 50% discount and the Fiji Visitors Bureau picked up the rest.

My story on the *Uluilakeba* appeared in four major Sunday papers. Hopefully it generated enough interest in Fiji to make up for the fact that I ignored other attractions.

Just 14 months later, on Dec. 10, 1973, the *Uluilakeba* capsized and sank during a cyclone with a loss of 54 lives.

French accent

My next stop was Noumea, capital of the French overseas territory of New Caledonia.

New Caledonia
Riviera of the Pacific

Try to picture a town from the French Riviera in a South Seas setting and you'll have a pretty good idea what Noumea is like.

Noumea has sidewalk cafés, tree-lined squares, discotheques, speeding Renaults, whitewashed houses hugging hillsides and a swanky yacht harbor. And due to its location halfway between Fiji and Australia, it also offers white sand beaches, rustling palms, blue lagoons and plenty of bikinis.

If the atmosphere seems decidedly European, it's because half of the more than 45,000 people who live in the city are French. The rest are native Melanesians, plus a few thousand Asians and Polynesians.

You might say New Caledonia is a small scale French equivalent of Australia. Both places began as penal colonies and evolved into lands of opportunity. New Caledonia now derives much of its income from the export of nickel ore, and many workers earn higher salaries than the average person back in France.

Noumea is situated near the southeastern tip of New Caledonia, a cigar-shaped island about 240 miles long and an average of 30 miles wide.

The most remarkable thing about the city is you don't have to travel far to find a good beach, as is the case in some other South Pacific capitals. There are two fine beaches – Anse Vata and Baie des Citrons – within three miles of the center.

Several hotels are located on or near the mile-long Anse Vata beach, including the island's most prestigious hostelry, the newly expanded 330-room Chateau Royale. Singles range from $26 to $45 and doubles run from $30 to $47.

A good choice among the lower-priced hotels is the Hotel Noumea at the Baie des Citrons, where the single tariff is $10-$14 and doubles are $20-$24.

Anse Vata is the site of Noumea's foremost attraction, the aquarium. What makes this one more interesting than most is the fact that it is stocked exclusively with fish and marine life from the nearby lagoon. A special feature is the luminescent coral which is on display only between 1:30 and 2:30 p.m. The aquarium is open daily except Monday and Friday. There is a small admission fee.

You have your choice of a number of excursions out of Noumea. Most popular is a trip to the Isle of Pines, some 70 miles to the south. The island gets its name from the many Norfolk Island Pines dotting the landscape.

Before I visited the island, I had read that the sand in some areas was as white and fine as talcum powder. I was surprised to find that was true.

Among the island's other attractions are the ruins of a prison that was used from 1871 to 1884.

The Isle of Pines has a pleasant hotel called the Relais de Kanumera, where bungalows rent for $20 single and $40 double, including meals.

Round trip airfare is $18. There are great views of submerged reefs along the way.

Closer to Noumea is Ile Ouen, an island off the south coast. It's a nice place but I preferred the Isle of Pines.

Another possible excursion is an all-day cruise to Phare Amedee, a Napoleanic era lighthouse that guards the entrance to Noumea's harbor. Three different boats make the trip and fares are less than $16 per person including a *pique-nique* lunch. You can swim at the lighthouse and buy souvenir coral.

The island of Ouvea, about 150 miles north of Noumea, has a fantastic 15-mile-long beach but the tourist office discourages visitors, citing poor accommodations.

A few venturesome travelers tour the quiet little towns on New Caledonia's east coast. Some even make the trip in rental cars, braving hundreds of miles of unpaved roads.

I flew up to two of the east coast towns – Hienghene and Touhu – and found little to rave about aside from an abundance of seashells along the beach. The houses and people were European and I saw little sign of native life. Only a dedicated scenery lover could appreciate a trip to this area.

New Caledonia, being French, has high prices, such as a charge of at least $2 for coffee and croissants in many hotels.

Taxis in Noumea tend to be expensive because they are dispatched with their meters ticking. I took a taxi once and wound up paying $2.30 for a half-mile ride. After that, I switched to little buses that go all over for 30¢.

You'll begin your visit by handing out $5 for the 35-mile bus ride between the international airport and Noumea. (Planes to internal destinations use a smaller, closer airport.) When you leave, you pay a $5 departure tax besides the bus fare.

Tourism is still in its youthful stage in New Caledonia. The only U.S. airline serving Noumea, Pan Am, flies in only once a week.

Government officials attribute a lack of tourists to an acute shortage of hotel rooms a few years back. However, the hotels have caught up and Noumea now awaits travelers who want to add a little French flavor to their South Pacific holiday.

I got off to a rocky start in Noumea by paying $1.75 for a cup of coffee. Even worse, the hotel I had written to seeking a discount, the Ile de France, didn't recall receiving my letter. When I finally got in touch with the manager, the best deal I could get was 50% off.

But everything quickly improved. The reservations manager at the Chateau Royale, the best hotel in town, arranged for a free room. I wasted no time in switching.

Next, all kinds of freebies came my way. The tourism

office got me a free flight to the Isle of Pines, where I had lunch at a nice hotel followed by a two-hour guided tour of the island in a Mini Moke beach buggy, accompanied by a *National Geographic* photographer named Dave Arnold.

I wish I had brought along a little bottle to scoop up some of the extra fine, glaringly white sand.

Back in Noumea, there was a lavish dinner with a group of Australian travel agents. Then there were more free excursions and meals, including a flight to the island of Ouvea, a boat trip with the travel agents to the old lighthouse and another flight to see parts of the east coast. I had hit the travel writer's jackpot.

Fortunately, I was able to reciprocate. My story appeared in Chicago, Toronto, LA and San Francisco, bringing New Caledonia to the attention of anyone who read the travel pages. The hotel and tourist office presumably got their money's worth.

New Zealand, quickly

The freebies all but dried up when I hit New Zealand, but I managed to get discounts of up to 50% on hotel rooms.

I quickly zipped through Auckland, Wellington and Christchurch, traveling by air. The cities had the look and feel of Britain as I imagined it had been 50 years earlier.

The men in Auckland wore dark suits and ties, teen-aged girls wore either long skirts or minis and little children were cherubic-looking with blue eyes and red cheeks.

Queen Street was the main drag and there were white lines painted down the middle of the sidewalks, apparently to keep pedestrians moving in an orderly fashion.

There were a great many Col. Sanders and Wimpy fast food outlets as well as health food stores.

Wellington seemed more spread out than Auckland. There were snack bars everywhere, mostly greasy spoon types, and young native Maoris sported Afro hairdos.

Despite miniskirts, many girls took on a matronly look around the age of 15.

Ornate wooden buildings, some with balconies, were being torn down to make way for concrete and glass skyscrapers.

Christchurch had more school uniforms than I'd ever seen anywhere. Other than that, blue jeans were very popular. Older people wore dark, heavy clothing even on warm days.

The Avon River, with its grassy bench-lined banks, curved through the city.

The Botanical Gardens were very pleasant with an endless variety of trees and flowers. Birds chirped, ducks frolicked in ponds and a little motor train chauffeured visitors.

Australia coast-to-coast

After somewhat stuffy New Zealand, Australia was much more appealing.

I did very well on freebies too. My biggest coup was arranging a free open ticket on Australia's largest independent airline, Ansett. I dropped by the airline office and was instructed to put my request in writing, which I did. It was approved the same day.

I was allowed to fly space available anywhere in the country. The ticket, written to my specifications, took me from Sydney to Adelaide to Alice Springs, then Darwin (by bus instead of plane), Brisbane, back to Sydney, cross-country to Perth, back east and south to Hobart on the island of Tasmania, then to Canberra, ending in Sydney.

The only time I got bumped was in Adelaide. I was already on the plane, standing in the aisle, when it was determined that all seats were filled. I returned to my hotel and was successful in boarding the next day.

The ticket, valued at $653.52 (U.S.), was my best single freebie ever. The Pan Am letter really paid off.

Unfortunately, Ansett went out of business in March 2002 after 66 years in the air.

I had hoped to travel across Australia on the Indian-Pacific train which runs between Sydney and Perth, but it was booked well in advance. Since I had no idea when I might get to Australia, I couldn't make a reservation. The trip covers 2,461 miles in three days and is regarded as one of the world's great rail journeys.

I didn't write any stories on the big cities but I did do a brief overview of the country.

<u>Australia</u>
A Thumbnail Sketch

Australia is California with a British accent.

There's no argument about the geography. Australia has beaches like Southern California (only better), mountains like the Sierra Nevada (only more) and deserts like the Mojave (only bigger).

The people of urban Australia have a stoic British exterior that camouflages an inner California casualness.

Like Californians, Australians love swimming, surfing, camping and outdoor life. They watch imported U.S. TV shows, shop at K Mart and eat Col. Sanders' chicken.

Like the British, they love afternoon tea, pubs and cricket. They dress conservatively (except on the beach) and read tabloid newspapers that print everything but the news.

Each city has its own character:

Sydney – Lively cosmopolitan city of skyscrapers and parks overlooking a beautiful harbor. Top attractions are the Opera House, the King's Cross nightlife area and 50 miles of beaches.

Melbourne – Sedate but bustling commercial center of the country known for its art museum. Streetcars and flower vendors give it a European atmosphere.

Brisbane – Relaxed, pleasant city with a subtropical climate. It's the gateway to the 1,200 mile long Great Barrier Reef and the Gold Coast, a Waikiki-style beach strip.

Canberra – Clean, spacious national capital with wide tree-lined boulevards and modern buildings. The Australian War Memorial, with its fine museum, is very impressive.

Alice Springs – Small, dusty desert town that retains a frontier feeling despite air conditioning. Tours to the awe-inspiring Ayers Rock originate here.

Hobart – Quiet, old fashioned city with a wealth of Georgian-style architecture. Historic prison ruins nearby and a waterfront gambling casino attract visitors.

Perth – Bright, sunny city of white buildings honeycombed with shopping arcades. Sights include magnificent beaches and Rottnest Island, home of little kangaroos called quokkas.

Adelaide – Unpretentious city noted for its parklands. Important vineyards are nearby. The renowned biennial Festival of Arts will be held this coming March.

Darwin – Hot, humid and rather dull. It's a departure point for wildlife safaris.

There were a few things I hadn't mentioned. One was to be on the alert for a very common Australian expression that might be confusing. If someone asks, "You all right?" it means, "May I help you?"

The working men's pubs often looked as if a bomb had gone off: smoky with littered floors and dazed expressions.

Adelaide seemed to have the greatest concentration of the shortest miniskirts, with Brisbane second. But the bikinis on the beaches made the miniskirted women look overdressed.

TV shows in Australia in the mid-70s included *McHale's Navy, Marcus Welby, I Dream of Jeannie, Mod Squad, Laugh In, Flip Wilson, Divorce Court, Jungle Jim, F Troop* and *Car 54, Where Are You?* They didn't miss much.

As noted in my article, the museum at the Australian War Memorial in Canberra was one of the best I'd seen anywhere. Everything was presented clearly, concisely, informatively and imaginatively. It couldn't have been better.

What impressed me most was a display showing how Australian troops covered their retreat from the ill-fated Gallipoli campaign in Turkey in 1915. They rigged up their rifles in the trenches to fire after they had left by running cords through a series of pulleys from the triggers to water-filled cans. The cans had holes punched in them. When a certain amount of water leaked out, each rifle fired.

The rock

It felt as if someone had opened an oven door as I stepped off the plane at Alice Springs following a three and a half hour propeller flight across the outback from Adelaide.

The town was surprisingly modern. A mixture of aborigines and men dressed like prospectors strolled the sidewalks of the four-block-long business district, which paralleled a dry river bed.

I quickly arranged a free round trip flight to Ayers Rock aboard a small airline called Connair. That resulted in a story that appeared in the *Boston Globe* on February 4, 1973.

Central Australia
Watching the Rock Watchers

It's a strange ritual.

One hour before dusk, half a dozen buses and cars loaded with people roll up to a predetermined spot in the vast central desert of Australia. The people get out and form an irregular line with everyone facing east. They keep their eyes pinned on a huge rust-colored rock that fills the horizon two miles away.

The people talk, shift their weight from one foot to the other and occasionally glance over their shoulders to check the progress of the setting sun. Slowly the rock begins to change color, from rust to orange to glowing red. Nikons and Instamatics start clicking. The colors keep changing, from vermillion to purple to mauve.

Finally, as darkness falls and the rock turns into a blue silhouette, the people file back to their buses and cars and disappear across the desert.

This is the nightly ritual at Ayers Rock, an oblong mass of sandstone that bears the distinction of being one of the largest rocks in the world, if not the most chameleonic. It stands 1,110 feet high, measures more than a mile from end-to-end and has a circumference of five miles.

Twilight picture-snapping isn't the only activity at the rock. Many visitors feel the urge to climb the imposing monolith. Hopeful conquerors set out at dawn to escape the heat of the day. They begin the climb at a specially marked area on the western slope.

A well-worn path leads to the summit, which is a one-mile hike from the base. The face of the rock slants at a 45-degree angle for most of the distance. In places where it's steeper, there's a heavy chain to hang on to. It takes at least 90 minutes to get up and back.

Not everyone who starts the climb has the courage to complete it. Some cover 100 yards or so, then decide they've had enough. They scoot back down in a sitting position.

There's no question that climbing the rock is dangerous. Two tourists have fallen to their deaths in the past 10 years. Plaques erected in their memory serve as subliminal safety reminders.

Tourists are free to scale the rock any time they desire, but the local folks try to discourage midday climbs, warning that the surface temperature can get as high as 150 degrees – or as one man put it – "hot enough to make rubber-soled shoes bubble."

If climbing the rock doesn't seem appealing, you can always walk around it. This takes about three hours. There are numerous caves to explore, many with ancient drawings on the walls.

In some spots, you see a gaping hole where the rock apparently has been dissolved away by a rare burst of rain. Black streaks mark the paths of phantom waterfalls.

One important thing about Ayers Rock that no one seems to mention is the millions of annoying flies that have deputized themselves as guardians of the rock. Potential hikers should load up on insect repellent. If you don't have any, the only other way to lose the flies is to retreat into a dark cave.

Ayers Rock is a national park. There isn't much there aside from a few motels, a general store and housing for park rangers.

Although thousands of tourists visit the rock every year, many others no doubt are deterred by the fact that it's located in the middle of nowhere and costs a few bills to reach. The only sizable town within nearly 800 miles is Alice Springs (population 11,500) and even it isn't very close. There's a standing joke about the tourist who gets off a plane in Alice, hops into a taxi and says, "Take me to the rock." He turns red when the driver tells him it's 297 unpaved miles away.

Alice Springs, however, is the starting point for tours to the rock.

Connair, a local airline, offers an overnight excursion from Alice for $85 that gives you 21 hours at the rock. The price includes all ground transport, park entrance fee, hotel room and meals.

Connair also has a day tour for $73 that allows seven hours at the rock. The problem with this tour is that you arrive too late for the morning climb and leave before the evening rock watch begins.

The most ridiculous thing I saw was a group of Europeans on a trip around the world who allotted only an hour and 15 minutes for the rock. They jumped off the plane, raced around the rock in a bus, then flew away.

Here's a good way to decide if a trip to the rock would be worthwhile. If you've ever been to the Grand Canyon and said, "Aw, it's just a big hole in the ground," then forget it. After all, Ayers Rock is just a big rock.

In addition to the *Boston Globe,* the *San Francisco Examiner, Toronto Star* and *Los Angeles Times* ran the piece. The Australian Tourist Commission bought it too.

Since Australia adopted a dual naming policy in 1993, Ayers Rock has also been known by its aboriginal name, Uluru. Ayers was Sir Henry Ayers, who served as premier of South Australia in the late 1800s. He didn't discover the rock. It was simply named after him.

The road north

Instead of flying between Alice Springs and Darwin, I covered the 934 miles by bus to get a look at the countryside from ground level.

The Pioneer Darwin Express rolled out of Alice Springs heading north at 3:45 p.m. with a driver in his 20s at the wheel. There were only 11 passengers occupying 38 seats. It was a cross section of young, old and in between. A little girl carrying a mouse in a shoebox wondered aloud if he would survive the trip. An old woman told her not to worry.

For the first few hours, the land was flat with a heavy growth of yellow grass. There were bushes and scattered trees, some of them white, and two foot high conical ant hills.

The roadway was red dirt, barely wide enough for the bus, which had to straddle the edge when a car came south.

After three hours, the terrain became slightly hilly with long plateaus in the distance and large red rocks near the road.

At sunset, the red dust brightened in color and the grass turned white as if frosty.

At 8:15 p.m., there was a 45 minute rest stop at the Wauchone Hotel, a combination hotel/bar/restaurant/gas station/store. There were five trucks parked in front and a pool table inside. Coffee and a ham sandwich cost less than $1.

Two and a half hours later, we stopped at a spot called Three Ways, where several bus routes came together. It was a dingy place with a long bar crowded with outback characters.

At Tennant Creek, Mile 310, many passengers left, including the girl with the mouse. Others got on. Tennant Creek was modern looking at night with a new movie theater and a bunch of aborigines standing around.

I slept most of the night. When I awoke around 7 a.m., there was a fresh driver and we were rolling through flat country headed for a town named Kathrine.

As we moved farther north, there were large termite mounds along the road plus pandanus shrubs and small palms.

Around 9, we stopped at Katherine, Mile 719, for 45 minutes for brunch. More passengers got on.

As we got closer to Darwin, the land became hilly with more vegetation. Arrival was at 2:15 p.m., 22 ½ hours after leaving Alice.

Darwin was very hot but most places were air conditioned. Many houses were on stilts. There were beaches too, but they weren't the greatest.

Penguins & other creatures

Continuing to cover subjects that other writers might have skipped, I did a piece on Australian animals focusing on penguins.

Phillip Island
Penguins Gain Popularity

Australia might be famous for its kangaroos and koalas but its penguins are nearly as popular.

For five months each year – from November through March – thousands of penguins return to Phillip Island, some 80 miles south of Melbourne, to nest and raise their young. Called fairy penguins, they stand just over one foot tall.

The female generally lays two eggs which take about five weeks to hatch. During the wait, both parents take turns going out to sea to feed on small fish and plankton.

After the chicks are hatched, the parents continue to share the babysitting duties. The one that goes fishing gorges itself with extra food which it later regurgitates to feed the young.

Different members of the colony go to sea each day, staying out for two or three days. Every morning some penguins leave and every evening others return.

Their nightly return has come to be known as the "penguin parade," and hundreds of curious humans turn out to watch the spectacle.

The humans are confined to a small grandstand. No camera flashes or loud noises are permitted because if the penguins are frightened they might cough up the extra food, causing their chicks to starve.

The penguins begin to pop out of the surf at sundown. Early arrivals stand in the water and wait a few minutes for others to appear. After several dozen are ready, the parade begins.

Soon there are penguins everywhere, waddling and stumbling toward their burrows, their paths lit by floodlights. The parade continues for more than an hour.

The best way to get to the penguin parade aside from renting a car is on a tour bus. I went on the Pioneer-Gray Line tour. The bus left Melbourne at 3 p.m. and returned shortly after 11. It cost less than $10, not counting food.

En route to the penguin beach, the bus stopped at a koala refuge on Phillip Island so passengers could get a good look at the little bear-like animals.

If you want to see more koalas, as well as kangaroos, emus and other native Australian animals, head for one of the wildlife sanctuaries located outside most major cities. The sanctuaries are small privately operated zoos designed to let visitors come in close contact with the animals.

There's one at Healesville, 39 miles southeast of Melbourne, called the Sir Colin MacKenzie Sanctuary. It has a wider variety of animals on display than many other sanctuaries. In addition to the usual koalas, kangaroos, wallabies (small kangaroos) and emus (Australian ostriches), you'll see dingos (wild dogs), wombats (burrowing marsupials), plenty of birds and even a duck-billed platypus.

The platypus swims around in a large aquarium. Since it's nocturnal, it's only shown twice daily, from 10:30 to 11:30 a.m. and 2 to 4:30 p.m.

Emus are allowed to roam around at will. There's also an open area where you can mingle with kangaroos. The emus, by the way, are always hungry and have been known to stick their heads in pockets or purses in search of food.

You can visit Healesville on a tour bus for less than $5.

There are three sanctuaries in the Brisbane area, one near Adelaide, one near Canberra and two in the vicinity of Sydney.

The Lone Pine Koala Sanctuary in suburban Brisbane is popular with tourists because they can have their picture taken holding one of the cuddly koalas. In addition, there's a large fenced area where visitors can feed handfuls of corn to friendly kangaroos and wallabies.

Lone Pine is easy to get to on your own either by bus or a pleasant riverboat ride. Transportation and admission charges come to around $3.

If you can't get to one of the sanctuaries, don't miss the Taronga Park Zoo in Sydney. Built on a terraced hillside across the harbor from the downtown area, it's regarded as one of the world's most beautiful zoos. It features all Australian animals as well as creatures from other parts of the globe. There's a regular cross-harbor ferry service for 25¢. Admission is $1.50.

As this was written, the zoo and the sanctuaries were still operating, although the prices certainly have increased. And the penguins were still waddling ashore at Phillip Island.

While I was in Australia, an off-year election was held in the United States.
A good friend, David Towell, was running for Nevada's lone congressional seat. I wanted to see how he did, so I stopped by the U.S. Information Service office in Sydney to ask about election results. I was directed to a teletype that was pumping out copy. As I stood reading it, Towell's name came across. He won.
I imagine my telegram congratulating him was the only one he received from Australia.

Instead of flying directly back to the U.S., I decided to stop in Fiji to gather material for a story about a hurricane that had roared through the islands one month earlier. It was an experiment to see if I could sell a semi-hard news story.
The storm, Hurricane Bebe, killed 20 people, left thousands homeless and caused $16 million in damage. The international airport at Nadi was closed for three days, stranding thousands of tourists.
Staying 24 hours at a hotel near the airport, I checked the progress of the cleanup efforts by speaking with people involved in hotels and tourism, collecting news releases from the Fiji Visitors Bureau and traveling to the nearby town of Lautoka to read the files at the *Fiji Times*.

That resulted in a story called "Fiji is Ready When You Are." Unfortunately, only one paper used it, the Sunday *Washington Star-News*. But since I managed to get a free hotel room, I probably didn't lose any money on the stopover.

The South Pacific-Australia trip was the only time I ever played the travel writer card, and I never would have thought of it if it hadn't been for the offer of a free hotel room in Tahiti.

My round trip plane ticket between LA and Australia was $1,479.50. Other expenses totaled $1,347 and I earned $1,305 from selling articles and photographs.

That means nearly four months in the South Pacific cost me $1,521.50.

I got well over $1,500 in freebies – maybe much more. I don't know the exact amount because I often got free flights, hotel rooms and sometimes meals everywhere but New Zealand, and in most cases I had no idea of the value.

As expected, I didn't get a penny from Pan Am. Although I did mention the airline a few times, I came nowhere close to fulfilling the agreement.

South America

Sailing down the Amazon

I had established myself as a travel writer before making my two trips across the Pacific.

I always admired the writers who filled the pages of the *Chicago Tribune's* big Sunday travel section. Trying to join their ranks would be a challenge, but since I was a writer who enjoyed traveling, it made sense to give it a shot.

To figure out how to do it, I studied articles to see how long they were and how they were written and formatted.

It was clear I couldn't simply write a story about London or Paris. That's been done too many times and a city is too broad a subject. I had to zero in on a certain aspect that may have been overlooked by other writers.

My part time career as a travel writer began after I left my full time job as a news producer at WBBM-TV (CBS) in the summer of 1970 and made a three-month swing through South America.

Although many people may think all of South America is the same, I noticed big differences from one region to another. Even within Brazil, which is larger than the continental United States, the Amazon basin had a frontier feeling, coastal cities such as Rio and Salvador had a certain *joie de vivre* and Sao Paulo was as cosmopolitan as New York City. Buenos Aires and Santiago, the capitals of Argentina and Chile, looked as if they'd been shipped over from Europe.

My very first story, describing a journey down the Amazon River, was published by the *Chicago Tribune* on January 17, 1971, along with two of my photos. It was a thrill to see it in print.

Brazil
Cruising the Amazon

Travelers who fly to one of the steamy cities along the Amazon probably do so because they want to get a close look at life in the rain forest from the deck of a meandering riverboat.

Anyone who does manage to spend a few days on the river will be treated to a rare experience. People may think the ships sail straight down the middle. Actually, they stay where the deepest water is, and it's usually on the outside of a curve, putting the ship almost within touching distance of the forest.

The Amazon is not a place for those who crave excitement. The atmosphere might best be described as tranquil. A century of river commerce has driven most of the dangerous animals and primitive Indians deeper into the wilderness.

Although the Amazon is home to the flesh-eating piranha fish and other savage creatures, all one is likely to see is a dolphin frolicking or a manatee grazing peacefully near the riverbank. The legendary warrior women have been replaced by quiet river people who eagerly paddle out to passing ships to trade a string of fish or bananas for old clothing or a bar of soap.

One memorable thing about the Amazon is the fantastic view of the heavens at night. After sunset, with the greenery pumping tons of fresh oxygen into the air, the sky becomes so clear that visitors from smoggy civilization marvel at the unexpected brilliance of the stars.

The cities of the Amazon still reflect some of the grandeur of the late 1800s when world demand for rubber brought instant prosperity to the area.

Gazing upon the weathered mansions in Manaus and Belém, it's not hard to imagine those golden days when the rubber barons ordered furniture, food and clothing from Europe.

The most splendid relic of that era is the opera house in Manaus, a stately building put together with Italian marble, Glasgow steel and ironwork from France. The opera house had its grand opening on New Year's Eve, 1896, and it's still being used today.

Manaus might have remained one of the most chic cities in the world if it hadn't been for Henry Wickham, an Englishman who walked off with a bunch of rubber seeds in 1876. Wickham and his associates began growing trees in Ceylon, and by 1911 Ceylon was outproducing and underselling the Amazon.

There are ships to fit any budget, though most are on the lower end of the scale. Ocean-going vessels can navigate as far upstream as Iquitos, Peru, some 2,300 miles from the Atlantic. Fares for this distance range from about $50 to $200. A fast ship traveling between Iquitos and Belém can make the trip nonstop in seven days. Going upstream against the current, it takes nine days.

If that seems like a long time, keep in mind that Francisco de Orellana – the first European to sail completely down the Amazon – needed eight months to make his way from the Andes to the sea.

Most of the traffic on the Amazon is between the coastal city of Belém and Manaus. Few large ships venture farther upstream than Manaus, which is nearly 1,000 miles from the Atlantic.

Aspiring travelers should be warned that catching a boat often requires a mixture of patience and determination. Unless a person is incredibly lucky, he should prepare a flexible itinerary that allows for at least one week of delays. No one hurries on the Amazon. Most shipping companies seem reluctant to reveal their sailing dates. Reservations are practically unheard of.

The company with the greatest number of ships on the river is the Brazilian government line ENASA which has three round trip voyages each month between Manaus and Belém. Each ship carries around 200 passengers in two classes: first and third. First class ticket holders ride in stuffy four-berth cabins while third class patrons bring their own hammocks and stake out swinging space on one of the rear decks.

The most comfortable way to travel the Amazon is on a three-class cruise ship operated by the Lloyd Braziliero line of Rio de Janeiro. These ships carry several hundred passengers and make one trip each month from Rio to Manaus and back.

Only one company sends ships all the way to Iquitos: the British-owned Booth Line. Booth has been sailing the Amazon since shortly after the river was opened to foreign traffic in 1866. A Booth freighter leaves New York for Iquitos at least once each month with space for four passengers.

Heading the roughing-it category is the JONASA line, a Brazilian company that usually dispatches one ship a month between Belém and Manaus. JONASA's ships are smaller than the others, having room for about 50 people in a dozen crude cabins, plus deck space for the hammock crowd.

Other ships of the JONASA type and smaller can be found by visiting the market section of each port. Any ship that's going anywhere has a sign on front listing its destinations as well as the date and time of departure.

The smaller ships call at more ports. Consequently the voyage lasts longer and passengers can see more. As might be expected, the quality of the food and accommodation usually declines in relation to the size of the ship.

For those who wish to travel farther upstream than Manaus, ENASA and JONASA occasionally send ships to the Peruvian-Colombian border and up the Madeira River to Porto Velho, a Brazilian town not far from Bolivia.

Sample fares for the Belém to Manaus run: ENASA, $33 for first class and $14 in third class; Booth, $80; Lloyd Braziliero, $100 in special first class, $72 for regular first class and $48 in tourist class; and JONASA, $30. All prices include meals.

Travel agencies in the principal cities offer excursions into the rain forest. The most popular tours are those conducted by Manuel "Bebé" Barros, who works out of the Lord Hotel in Manaus. Bebé has an all-day excursion for $10 that includes swimming and piranha fishing (not at the same time), plus a visit to the spot where the yellow-ochre waters of the Amazon meet the black waters of the Rio Negro. The two mighty rivers flow side-by-side for several hundred feet before mixing.

The hotels of Amazonia don't quite measure up to their official ratings. Hot water and air conditioning are a rarity.

Single rooms in the best hotels list for $10 to $15 a day. These include the Grand

Para in Belém, the Lord and the Amazonas in Manaus, the Iquitos (also known as the Turista) in Iquitos and the Parador Ticuna in Leticia, Colombia.

The Parador Ticuna, better known as Mike's Place, is the newest hotel on the Amazon. It's run by Mike Tsalickis, a Greek-American animal exporter from Florida who injected life into Leticia and earned it a place on the map. You may have heard of Mike. He's the guy who likes to wrestle 35-foot anaconda snakes and always wins – so far.

Since Leticia is literally in the middle of nowhere, Mike's hotel is an attraction in itself. It has a dozen motel-style rooms built around what must be the only swimming pool within hundreds of miles. Each room has a private bath, a bar, a mini-refrigerator, a screened patio with two hammocks and, of course, a slow-turning ceiling fan.

Mike offers all kinds of excursions including a $200 a day jaguar hunt.

Less expensive hotels in each city have single rooms for anywhere between $1.50 and $7. A few of them are the King in Belém, the Central and the Rio Mar in Manaus and the Imperial in Iquitos.

Two restaurants popular with foreigners are the Kavala Pizzeria in Manaus and the Caravelle in Iquitos.

For snack bar fans, there's the Go-Go Luncheonette in Manaus, where modern day Amazons in miniskirts sip chocolate shakes made from powdered milk and double-filtered water.

Weatherwise, it's hot and humid along the Amazon all year. Although the rainy season falls during the winter, it can rain any day, and often does, for an hour or two.

Looking at the story today, the lead was dull, it was wordy, too long and fizzled out at the end. But after all, it was my first attempt, and I was trying to write for people who might want to make the trip themselves.

Although three other papers printed the piece besides the *Trib*, the travel editor at the *Washington Post* rejected it, complaining it lacked adventure. He was right. The only adventure I could think of would have been being attacked by pirates or piranhas. I'm glad neither happened.

Amazon footnotes

My story made everything sound easier than it really was. Due to normal breaks in travel as well as delays, it took me three weeks to get down the Amazon.

I began my voyage at Iquitos because that was as far as ocean-going ships could travel. I started by flying from Chicago via Miami to Bogotá, then waiting overnight in the airport for a flight to Leticia – 680 miles to the south. The final leg took five hours in a DC-4.

Since Leticia was smack in the middle of the rain forest, I started taking quinine before leaving the U.S. to reduce the chances of contracting malaria. I stayed at Mike's Place. A girl who worked there told me the mosquitoes didn't come inside the town limits because the area had been sprayed, so I didn't need the tablets. Figuring the mosquitoes were unaware of exactly where the town limits were, I continued taking quinine and never got malaria.

Mike Tsalakis had a well-organized operation, starting with sending a minibus to the airport to solicit guests such as me. (I was aware of his hotel beforehand.) He also conducted tours to nearby places such as a shabby Indian village.

I was in Leticia for three days waiting for a flight upriver to Iquitos, where I would begin my river journey. I had to go there because Leticia was not a scheduled stop for the Booth Line. After getting to Iquitos, it was three more days before I could board the ship that would take me to Manaus. There, I planned to switch to a smaller ship to experience how the Brazilians traveled.

Although Iquitos was considerably larger than Leticia – a city, actually – it was also a quiet spot in the rain forest that had no roads to the outside world. Boats and planes were the only way in or out.

Trying to change money on my arrival was my first experience in dealing with financial oddities in South America. As I later wrote in an article entitled "South America Money Game":

> It was mid-afternoon on the day before a holiday, and I had no Peruvian soles. The airport *Cambio* (currency exchange) was closed, so I persuaded a taxi driver to take me into Iquitos for a few Colombian pesos.
>
> I checked into a hotel and tried to change money at the reception desk. The clerk said such a thing was absolutely forbidden. He told me I must go to a certain bank and instructed me on how to find it.
>
> I got to the bank 30 minutes before closing. Half a dozen tourists who arrived on the same plane were already lined up at one window waiting to change money. One young woman was taking care of them while several other tellers stood around doing nothing.
>
> Each transaction took about 10 minutes. Several forms had to be filled out, then initialed by three different bank officials.
>
> When my turn finally came, it was 20 minutes past closing time. The teller pointed to the clock and recommended I return in two days. I refused to leave, telling her I was getting hungry and needed some soles.
>
> After several minutes of debate, the problem was solved when the teller next to her offered to cash my check with money from his own pocket.

After the holiday, I located the office of the Booth Line and bought a ticket to Manaus for $100 plus $11 tax.

I got a financial jolt when checking out of my hotel, the Hotel Iquitos. I thought I had set aside enough soles to cover the bill, but they added two taxes and a service charge, boosting it by 23%. I had to rush back to the bank to change more money.

Lesson learned: find out in advance what the total will be. I also made it a point to have extra U.S. $1 and $5 bills to cover unexpected adjustments to the final hotel bill or taxi ride.

To reach the ship, a car from the steamship company took me about five miles outside Iquitos to a town called Bellavista. There, I boarded a small boat and traveled upriver for half an hour to a sawmill where the vessel was loading plywood. The ship was the 1,312 ton *Atahualpa,* named after the Inca emperor who was executed in 1533 by Spanish forces led by Francisco Pizarro. His death led to the collapse of the Inca Empire.

I got on the ship Friday night and arrived in Manaus Wednesday morning, the journey taking four full days.

Although there was no swimming pool, shuffleboard or casino because the ship was a freighter, just standing on deck watching the rain forest go by was entertainment enough. As the only passenger, I also got to visit the wheelhouse to learn something about navigating.

The trip was relaxing, the food was good and the cabin comfortable.

I was in Manaus for a week; longer than expected because I was waiting for the next ship. The day I arrived, I visited the ENASA office and learned they had a ship leaving for Belém in three days. Those three days ballooned into five.

I walked around Manaus until my feet were sore, checking out the famous opera house, the zoo and other sights. I occasionally shared drinks or meals with three other characters I had run into: Bebé, the Brazilan who ran a travel agency, an American who operated a gift shop and a visiting American who taught school in Rio.

I was to be sailing on a ship named the *Augusto Montenegro*. Not surprisingly, there was a false start. After I checked out of my hotel and lugged my bags to the dock, I was told to return in the morning.

The next day, the ship was supposed to sail at 8 p.m., so I was allowed to board during the day. It actually left at 1:30 the next morning.

My $17.80 first class ticket got me a bed in a four-bunk cabin with three Italian guys, one of whom was very hyper and noisy. There were about a dozen other foreigners on the ship, mostly Americans, Germans and a few Swiss. As mentioned in my article, the locals tended to travel deck class.

Unlike the huge oceangoing ship that couldn't dock in most places, the smaller vessel stopped a number of times at various towns. Passengers could get off and look around, wandering through riverside markets stocked with fish, bananas and other staples.

On the minus side, the food aboard the ship wasn't very good. One meal featured spaghetti with meatballs and sand.

We sailed for four solid days. On the second day, while docked at the city of Santarem, a barge was attached to the side of the ship where it remained for the rest of the voyage.

On the next to last day, we stopped around noon at a spot about six to eight hours short of Belém. A few of the passengers went swimming. Apparently the piranhas liked shallower waters. Word was there was a storm in Belém and the barge might be ripped loose or sunk if we got caught in it. The storm eventually passed by around 9 p.m. The ship moved on at 4 a.m. As we neared the coast, the river was so wide in spots that it was difficult to see the banks.

We were able to disembark shortly before noon. Belém was a large, bustling city – the only one I've ever visited, except for areas near military bases, where prostitutes openly approached men on the street.

Traveling companions

I wound up hanging out with two Germans I met on the boat, Juergen and Joachim, who were exploring South America after leaving teaching jobs in Colombia. In fact, I spent the next two months with one or both of them, traveling down the east coast of South America to the southern tip, then up the west coast.

They were average looking guys. Juergen had brown hair. Joachim had black hair and a full mustache.

One thing I learned from them was to be cordial when talking to people such as clerks in stores – something that's common in Europe but seldom practiced in the United States.

They pointed out that an American might walk into a shop and simply say, "Do you have…" or "I want such-and-such …," whereas a European would say, "Good morning. How are you? I have a question."

Juergen wanted to see Brasilia, the inland capital, and Joachim and I wanted to visit the coast, so we split up temporarily. Juergen took the bus for the 1,000 mile journey.

Joachim and I headed to the coastal city of Recife, also about 1,000 miles away. But rather than travel by bus, we bought plane tickets. Prior to boarding, each passenger was patted down by hand, something that was not uncommon in South American airports. The plane was a propeller-driven puddle-jumper that took seven and a half hours to get to Recife, stopping four times along the way.

A crowded carnival added excitement to the city. We were there for two and a half days, the time largely dependent on how soon we could catch a bus to Salvador.

While waiting, we used local buses to visit one of the beaches as well as an old city called Olinda, five miles out of town, only to get rained out each time.

Leaving on a bus in the rain at 10 p.m., it was very difficult to sleep. There were 36 passengers besides us, including an Englishman who was working in Uruguay.

After a 5:40 a.m. stop for breakfast, the bus got only two blocks before someone driving a jeep ran into the side of it, then drove off.

We traveled only a few more blocks before coming to the Sao Francisco River, where trucks, cars and buses were lined up waiting to be ferried across on one of three boats. The driver let two boats get away. He apparently was waiting for the jeep driver to be caught, and it looked as if he had been.

We would have encountered many more river crossings if we had traveled overland from Belém to Recife. That's one reason we flew.

We arrived in Salvador at mid-afternoon, only half an hour behind schedule despite the delays. As usual, our first task was to find a hotel. Fortunately, I had a recommendation from the American teacher in Manaus, a place called the Anglo-Americano. It was always good to have a hotel in mind rather than depend on the tourist office or guide books.

Salvador was a lively and colorful city known for its Portuguese colonial architecture and pastel-hued homes. It was the third largest city in Brazil after Sao Paulo and Rio. The population was predominantly Afro-Brazilian.

The city's official name was Salvador da Bahia, short for Salvador da Bahia de Todos os Santos, which means Holy Savior of All Saints Bay. With a name like that, it's no wonder most of the inhabitants were Catholic.

Leaving Salvador for Rio, the next bus was surprisingly nice. It had large folding seats like dentist chairs that made the 25-hour trip relatively comfortable. Hostesses ran up and down the aisle handing out Cokes and coffee and candy and crackers as well as a coupon for a meal at the rest stop. And there were only 19 passengers.

Rio!

Once in Rio, Joachim and I caught up with Juergen, who had already arrived. They roomed together and I got a single.

We were there for a week, running around to all the sights such as Corcovado, the 2,300 foot granite peak from where a statue of Christ the Redeemer watches over the city, and 1,300 foot Sugar Loaf Mountain.

Sugar Loaf was reached by taking two cable cars in succession. To illustrate how prices have changed – and this is staggering – tickets for those cable cars cost us a total of $1.32. I recently saw the price quoted at more than $20.

Prices in general were very reasonable in Brazil and elsewhere in South America. We never paid more than a few dollars for a room. In Rio, we frequented a snack bar called Gordon's, where a sub sandwich or kangaroo burger (double cheeseburger) cost little more than $1.

The Brazilian cruzeiro was worth a little less each day, so it was wise to buy only what was needed. I could always get a better rate the next day. (In 1994, the cruziero was replaced by a new currency, the real.)

We checked out world famous beaches such as Ipanema, Copacabana and Flamengo where itsy-bitsy teeny-weeny bikinis were *de rigueur*. The people were so crazy about the beaches that one day Copacabana was crowded despite a heavy fog.

One thing that amazed me was seeing Afro-Brazilian women as black as coal sitting on the beach slathering on sun tan lotion. Much like Honolulu, the people of Rio were a mixture of every possible combination of colors and races.

The three of us moved on to Sao Paulo, where Joachim met up with his Colombian girlfriend and quickly disappeared.

Sao Paulo, the largest city in the southern hemisphere, was a modern sprawling metropolis even then. The most interesting spot Juergen and I visited was the Buntantan Institute, which produced vaccines and snake serums. It had a nice museum with live snakes on display.

From there, we continued moving south by bus, stopping at Iguaçu Falls, one of the largest and most spectacular waterfalls in the world. It's situated at the spot where Brazil, Paraguay and Argentina meet.

I'd never heard of Iguaçu until I got to South America. The most exciting thing about that stop was a boat ride into the Devil's Throat, a raging cataract measuring 300 feet high, 500 feet wide and nearly half a mile long.

In the sleepy Paraguayan capital of Asunción, Juergen and I checked with our respective embassies to see if we needed visas for any upcoming countries. Although the answer was no, I was urged to think twice about going to Uruguay because the Tupamaro guerrillas had been pulling off political kidnappings and generally fomenting revolution.

We went anyway, flying to Montevideo on the Uruguayan national airline PLUNA. We flew because we got a better deal. A train would have cost $30 and taken two and a half days vs. $28 and two and a half hours for the plane, a Vickers Viscount turboprop. We never seriously considered the bus, which would have cost $16.

The only threat we experienced was not guerrillas but bad colds. We both had them. In fact, Juergen didn't even get out of bed one day. It was winter and getting cooler as we neared the bottom of the world. The chill and occasional rain didn't make it any easier to shake the colds.

With its broad, tree-lined streets and sidewalk cafés, Montevideo was a pleasant city with a European atmosphere.

I worked in a four-hour round trip bus ride to Punta del Este, an elegant resort known as the Riviera of South America. The sun came out long enough to enjoy the city.

We moved on to Buenos Aires, traveling about 140 miles up the Rio de la Plata from Montevideo on a large ship named *Ciudad de Formosa,* which carried more than 450 passengers. Our $6.70 second class tickets got us bunks in a nine-berth cabin. It wasn't as crowded as I had expected because not every bunk was filled.

The overnight journey took 10 hours. We arrived just in time to see the sun burn through the morning haze.

Like Montevideo, Buenos Aires also had wide boulevards and European-looking buildings. The city could have passed for parts of Paris or Vienna.

As a great beef producing nation, steaks were cheap and plentiful. At almost any little restaurant, we could get a T-bone with fries, a baguette and a glass of wine for $2 or $3, served by a waiter wearing a black suit with a white napkin draped over his arm.

Juergen and I both hoped to get to Tierra del Fuego, the large island shared by Chile and Argentina at the southern tip of the continent. On the way, we planned to travel through the lower third of Chile by ship.

First, we crossed the Andes by train to Santiago. (More on that train later.) The Chilean capital had as much a European look and feel as Buenos Aires and Montevideo, and the prices were just as reasonable. Besides, Chile was the only country we visited that had a black market for currency, so we saved a little that way.

We took in some of the sights in Santiago such as the Natural History Museum and watched people in a nearly park play shell games and hamster roulette. We couldn't find out much about ships down south except that one supposedly was in dry dock for its annual checkup.

One of my travel guides recommended a burlesque theater called Picaresque. I went to the 11 p.m. performance and was surprised to see it was an old fashioned vaudeville show. Strippers alternated with acts such as marimba players, jugglers and slapstick comedians. I had the feeling I was in the middle of a flashback, watching something that might have been staged decades earlier in the United States.

The theater was huge and I was seated far off on the left, allowing me to see behind the proscenium on the right. As one young stripper was being introduced over the PA, she stood fidgeting, then did a quick sign of the cross before strutting onstage.

I also saw the Robert Altman film *M·A·S·H* in Santiago. I couldn't imagine what the Chileans thought of it.

Striking out

Juergen and I traveled south by train to Puerto Montt, the last town on solid land before Chile broke up into a 1,000-mile-long archipelago stretching almost to the Antarctic. Although the archipelago was sparsely populated, hundreds of islands provided what promised to be fantastic scenery.

As we moved farther south, the land started looking like Wisconsin, with dairy cows munching grass on rich green hillsides. There were so many Germans in the area that German was said to be the first language.

We arrived in Puerto Montt on a rainy Sunday afternoon and checked into a nice little hotel called the Hotel Montt, overlooking the dock area. I set out to explore the town and walked from end to end in 15 minutes.

The next day, we learned there was a ship leaving Wednesday called the *Navarino*, although one crewman said it probably wouldn't really sail until Thursday. We looked the ship over. It was rusty on the outside but not bad inside. Good enough for us. We bought tickets.

While waiting, Juergen and I spent time traveling independently by bus to nearby towns or just hanging around Puerto Montt. One evening, we went to the local movie theater to see the Greek film *Z*, which was baffling for me because it was in French with Spanish subtitles.

When inquiring about the ship on Wednesday, we were surprised to learn the crewmen had gone on strike. One man said the strike would only last two or three days. There was one good sign: cargo was being loaded.

On Thursday, the strike was still in effect and no one knew how long it might last, so Juergen and I decided to forget about the ship. That was a strike for us too: Strike One.

We got our money back, went to the LAN Chile airline office and bought tickets to Punta Arenas, a city across the Strait of Magellen from Tierra del Fuego. That's where we had planned to wind up if the ship had sailed. The plane fare was less than the boat tickets but we lost out on the scenery.

We spent four and a half hours on a turboprop, arriving in Punta Arenas at nightfall. We checked into a small hotel one block away from the main plaza, the Hotel de France, getting a double with an airline-sized bathroom.

Visiting travel agencies the next morning, we learned there was a ferryboat and a plane that went across the strait to a town called Porvenir, but no one knew anything about buses leaving from there.

Juergen and I decided to take a chance. We bought tickets for the ferry, which appeared to be a large former military landing craft. The front end could be lowered to serve as a ramp. It was large enough to hold several big rigs.

The boat left late because trucks being loaded got bogged down in sand and had to be extracted by a Caterpiller snow plow. We departed just before noon for the two and a half hour trip. It was cold and windy and the sea was rough.

During the crossing, Juergen and I cornered three truck drivers and asked about getting a ride across the island to the Argentine side. One said he wasn't going that far. The others said they already had passengers.

Once ashore, we approached two young men in a pickup truck and asked for a ride into Porvenir, about three miles inland. They drove us to the bus depot, where we learned the bus only left on Tuesdays. It was Saturday and we were in the middle of nowhere.

That was Strike Two.

We convinced the guys in the pickup to take us back to the boat. If nothing else, the boat's hot coffee hit the spot.

We were determined to see more of Tierra del Fuego than the boat ramp and the little town of Porvenir.

Back in Punta Arenas, we dropped our stuff at our former hotel, where the clerk wasn't sure he had a room.

Our next goal was to get to Ushuaia, an Argentine town on the south coast of Tierra del Fuego. There were no direct flights there, so I suggested we check on buses.

At the bus station, we learned there was a departure in the morning to Rio Gallegos, about 150 miles away in Argentina, but we couldn't buy a ticket until we got cleared by the police. We did that quickly and wound up with tickets for $2.54 at the black market rate.

After checking another hotel just in case, a room opened up at the Hotel de France. We had hamburgers, then crashed.

Our bus left five minutes early, at 8:55 a.m. The road was covered with snow at first, causing some fishtailing, but it eventually became clear. After a midday rest stop at an isolated house, we crossed through both Chilean and Argentine customs. The land became perfectly flat.

Seven and a half hours after leaving Punta Arenas, we arrived in Rio Gallegos and checked into a hotel called the Alonso. There wasn't much to the town. It was Sunday afternoon and the airline office was closed, so we grabbed omelets at a nearby restaurant, then called it a day. We didn't even ask about a bus.

The next day, we changed money and bought plane tickets to Ushuaia. The good news was the plane ticket cost only $9.25. The bad news was that there wasn't a flight for two days and Rio Gallegos was a very quiet town. I burned up time by sleeping late, washing clothes in the hotel sink, writing letters and reading.

Tierra del Fuego

We flew south over the Strait of Magellan in a prop plane, watching the flat terrain change into snow-covered mountains. Arriving in Ushuaia, we took a bus into town and checked into the Hotel Albatross.

Ushuaia claimed to be the southernmost city in the world. Across the strait on the Chilean island of Navarino, a town called Puerto Williams boasted the same title. Although it was actually farther south, Puerto Williams was considered too small to be a contender because it was a tiny settlement of mostly military families.

We spent 48 hours in Ushuaia. On the second morning, with fresh snow on the ground, Juergen walked out of town far enough to get away from all sound. He said it was the first time he had ever experienced total silence and it was a very strange feeling.

I wrapped up the Tierra del Fuego experience in an article printed in Chicago, Los Angeles and San Francisco. The *Trib* ran it on March 28, 1971.

Tierra del Fuego
As Far as You Can Go

If the Earth really did have corners, Tierra del Fuego would be one of them.

This sprawling island at the bottom of South America is about as far south as anyone can go and still be standing on a sizable hunk of dry land.

The fact that it is so remote – some 1,400 miles from either Santiago or Buenos Aires – seems to attract veteran travelers and adventurers rather than regular tourists. There isn't much reason to be discouraged by the distance, however, because anyone who gets as far south as Santiago or B.A. can fly down to Tierra del Fuego and spend a few days in the best hotels for around $200.

The Chile-Argentina border runs right down the middle of the island, which is roughly half the size of Indiana and ranks as the 18th largest island in the world.

The northern part is grassy, treeless tableland punctuated by oil wells and grazing sheep. The southern half is dominated by the last of the Andes, a spur of 3,500 foot-high mountains that curl around the tip of the continent like an alligator's knobby tail.

Ushuaia, with a population of 6,000, is the largest settlement on the island. Perched on the slopes of snow-capped peaks, Ushuaia is a town of brightly painted wooden houses overlooking the Beagle Channel, a waterway named for the ship that carried Charles Darwin to Tierra del Fuego in 1832.

The first European settlers started moving onto the island only 100 years ago, so there's still something of a frontier atmosphere in the area. But that doesn't mean visitors have to rough it – Ushuaia has a fairly new first class hotel called the Albatross where the tab for a spacious double is $10.50.

There are several duty-free shops in Ushuaia specializing in items such as Japanese radios, British woolen goods and American cigarettes. A couple of stores also have vast displays of gaudy chinaware including Japanese tea sets and, of all things, tiny busts of George Washington.

Ushuaia derives a good part of its income from the Argentine navy and air force. The navy beds down in a former prison on the east end of town.

The principal Chilean city in the area

is Punta Arenas, located on the mainland across the Strait of Magellan. There's a statue in the central plaza honoring Ferdinand Magellan, who discovered the strait on his round the world voyage of 1520.

It was Magellan who gave Tierra del Fuego its name – Land of Fire – because of Indian fires he saw burning along the coast.

Punta Arenas is about 10 times larger than Ushuaia but similar in character. Its number one hotel is the Cabo de Hornos (Cape Horn), a modern skyscraper towering above the city center. A good second choice – with smaller rooms, thinner walls and lower prices – is the Hotel de France, which happens to be run not by a Frenchman but a man with a Yugoslavian surname.

There's nothing unusual about non-Spanish names in this part of South America. A great many people from central Europe migrated to southern sections of Chile and Argentina in recent decades, adding a strong Continental flavor to the area.

Although most tourists probably visit Tierra del Fuego just because of where it is, they find there's no shortage of spectacular scenery to keep them busy snapping pictures.

During the summer (North American winter), travel agencies in both Ushuaia and Punta Arenas conduct excursions to nearby lakes and glaciers.

Buses operate between various points on the island during most of the year. Bus service is nearly nonexistent in the winter, however, even though the roads are open most of the time.

The winters in Tierra del Fuego are actually milder than in the northern United States, although it's true that summer never really arrives. It rarely gets any warmer than the upper 50s.

Considering the weather, you might expect to find penguins wandering around the outskirts of Ushuaia. This is penguin country all right, but they prefer to live by themselves.

Actually there's a better chance of running into a flamingo. Plenty of them live near the Strait of Magellan.

Despite the penguin's shyness, he's the unofficial bird of Tierra del Fuego. In Ushuaia you can buy penguin postcards (shot in Antarctica). In Punta Arenas there's a bus company called the Penguin Express and a beer named Polar that features a swaggering penguin on its label.

With plane fares lower in Chile, it costs less to fly to Tierra del Fuego from Santiago than Buenos Aires.

There are several nonstop jets each week between Santiago and Punta Arenas, but getting to Ushuaia isn't quite so easy. Anyone heading there from either Santiago or Buenos Aires must change planes in Rio Gallegos, Argentina.

People visiting the Argentine ski resort of Bariloche can take a plane or bus across the Andes to Puerto Montt, then continue on to Punta Arenas by plane or ship.

The ship sails at least once a month and the journey lasts about a week. Ports of call include isolated villages in Chile's rugged fjord country. The one-way fare is about $55 – more than the plane – but the trip is reputed to be one of the greatest travel adventures in South America.

There's one added incentive for visiting Tierra del Fuego. Once you get this far south, you're also in Patagonia, so you can add two strange names to your travel log for the price of one.

I should have mentioned that finding a ship in Puerto Montt could be rather iffy.

We backtracked through Rio Gallegos and Punta Arenas and flew to Santiago. Juergen and I finally split up after traveling together for most of two months when he left one morning to head to Antofagasta in northern Chile. I spent part of my time getting visas for Bolivia and Ecuador.

I checked with LAN, the Chilean airline, about going to Easter Island, located more than 2,100 miles off the coast. The island, home to the giant stone heads called *moai,* has been administered by Chile since 1881.

The airfare of at least $200 wasn't bad. (The last time I checked, it was $800.) The problem was there was only one flight a week, meaning I could stay for either one day or eight. Of course one was too short and eight was too long.

Instead of going, I bought an Easter Island souvenir, a 10-inch high stone head, supposedly carved there, for about $5.

Looking back, I should have gone to Easter Island when I had the chance. As Yogi Berra famously said, "When you get to a fork in the road, take it."

Riding the rails to Lake Titicaca

My next stop was Arica, at the northern tip of Chile, only 11 miles south of the Peruvian border. I must have been burned out after two months on the road because I never thought of taking the bus or train from Santiago. I flew.

With annual rainfall at a fraction of an inch, Arica was said to be one of the driest places on Earth.

It was the jumping off point for a memorable journey that traversed three countries and included a boat ride across the highest lake in the world – a trip I described in an article printed by the *Chicago Tribune* on May 9, 1971.

Rolling Adventure
South America by Rail

A South American train is more than simply a means of getting from one place to another – it can be anything from a rolling adventure to a movable purgatory.

Fortunately, the trains tourists are likely to use are somewhat better than the rest with an edge on cleanliness and comfort.

The main thing that separates the good trains from the bad is speed. Ordinary trains are so slow they can make a fast-living gringo glassy-eyed. Even the express trains are slow by international standards, but anyone willing to sacrifice a little time will be rewarded with unique travel experiences.

One of the most fascinating journeys is a combination of two rail trips that takes you from the arid north coast of Chile through part of Bolivia to Cuzco, the ancient Inca capital high in the Peruvian Andes.

The first leg of the 550-mile excursion begins at Arica, a sun-kissed port where Chileans gather to swim, relax on the beach or gamble in the city's elegant casino.

You board a one-car diesel train called an autowagon for a nine and a half hour ride to La Paz, Bolivia. The train leaves every Wednesday morning. The one-way first class fare, which includes lunch, is less than $14.

Leaving Arica, the autowagon zigzags up through the coastal mountains to the Bolivian *altiplano*, a bleak, treeless plateau situated more than two miles above sea level. Along the way you pass walled Indian villages and herds of llamas tended by women in bowler hats.

For those who've never seen a llama outside a zoo, it's a real kick to watch dozens of them prancing along, staring arrogantly at the train.

At the eastern edge of the *altiplano,* the autowagon starts winding its way down the rim of a huge basin and you see La Paz stretched out below, looking like a scale model city in a punch bowl.

La Paz is one of the least visited capitals in South America but it's an interesting city with a large Indian population and some of the lowest prices on the continent.

The next leg of the trip is a 28-hour journey that includes a boat ride across Lake Titicaca, the highest lake in the world (altitude: 13,500 feet). The first class fare is $25. There are two departures a week, Wednesday and Friday.

After exploring La Paz, you hop on a train for a four hour ride to the lake. Here, at the port of Guaqui, you transfer to a steamer for an overnight crossing to Puno, Peru.

There are two steamers, both made in England in the early 1900s. Since Lake Titicaca has no outlet to the sea, the ships were carried up the mountains in pieces, then reassembled.

I sailed on the 260-foot *Ollanta,* the newer and better of the two. It's clean and has good meals which are included in the fare. Passengers sleep in bathless two-berth cabins.

It's wise to board the ship as soon as possible because berths are assigned on a first-come, first-served basis. If there are more passengers than beds, which has been known to happen, the extra people end up sleeping on couches in the dining room.

There were only 12 passengers including me, and only one was a South American – a middle-aged woman from Argentina. The roster went like this: five North Americans, including three Peace Corps volunteers based in Peru, a Dutch couple teaching school in Surinam, two French girls, an Englishman and a Cuban-born Spaniard working in Bolivia.

The French girls had second class tickets, meaning they were supposed to sleep on deck. They didn't want to, so the Spanish gentleman spent most of the evening negotiating for them with the captain and the steward. He eventually persuaded them to let the mademoiselles have an empty cabin at no extra cost.

It's worth hitting the deck early to see the rising sun cast a golden glow across the lake as solitary fishermen drift about in their famous reed boats.

After breakfast, the ship docks in Puno where you switch to a long, long train that gets you to Cuzco in 10 or 11 hours. Lunch is served en route for an extra $1.40.

As the train rumbles through the outskirts of Puno, you may catch a glimpse of Indians making boats in the reed beds along the shore.

At major stops during the day, you'll find Indian women selling knitted ponchos, rugs, pottery, llama dolls and tiny silver llamas, plus other trinkets. Some women board the train to look for customers. Many have displays on the station platforms.

For most of the trip, the railway parallels the Urubamba River, one of the tributaries of the Amazon.

Shortly after sunset, you arrive in Cuzco, once the most important city in the hemisphere, from where the Incas ruled a vast domain stretching from Ecuador to Argentina.

For people traveling in the other direction, the Cuzco-La Paz train leaves on Monday and Wednesday and the La Paz-Arica train departs every Thursday.

Cuzco, besides being a great attraction in itself, is also the gateway to the lost city of Machu Picchu, one of the most fabulous sights on Earth.

There's a daily express train to Machu Picchu at 7:15 a.m. It takes about three hours to get there. The return train heads back to Cuzco at 3:15. Round trip fare is $4.10.

Counting all the traveling time, including a 20-minute microbus ride from the train station to the ruins, you wind up with only three hours to explore Machu Picchu – just enough time for a quick once-over.

Those who prefer a more leisurely visit can stay overnight in the small government-run hotel near the ruins. It's nearly always full, so reservations are required.

Another worthwhile expedition is a journey through the Andes on a narrow-gauge railway that goes between Mendoza, Argentina and Los Andes, Chile with connections to Buenos Aires and Santiago.

The entire 900-mile trip takes up to 28 hours and costs from $25 to $45, depending on how much comfort you want. Departures are planned so the longest and least interesting part of the trip – the 15 hour stretch from Buenos Aires to Mendoza – takes place at night. There are four trains a week.

The running time from Mendoza to the top of the Andes is about five hours. The mountains grow from rolling foothills to soaring snow-capped peaks as the train skims along desolate slopes and darts through tunnels and snow sheds. On steep inclines, the engineer lowers a special cogwheel that helps pull the train uphill or keep it from going too fast downhill.

At mid-afternoon, shortly after crossing the summit, the train arrives at the fashionable Portillo ski resort, a good place to stop whether you ski or not.

Portillo is not a town – just a hotel complex and a train station. The hotel sleeps more than 550 people. Prices range from about $10.50 for a bathless room with two double bunks to $84 a day for a deluxe suite. All rates include meals.

Almost everything you could want is here – shops, laundry, movie theater, game room and outdoor swimming pool.

There are seven ski runs, the longest being a two mile slope with a vertical drop of 2,400 feet. At least one doctor is always on duty to treat casualties. Portillo averages one broken leg a day.

For après-ski activities, guests have their choice of a vibrating discotheque or a cozy bar complete with fireplace.

The winter sports season lasts from June through September.

Other notable South American rail trips include:

In Ecuador, a 12-hour roller coaster-type ride between mountain-bound Quito and tropical Guayaquil.

In Columbia, a one-day trip from Bogotá along the Magdalena River to the Caribbean resort of Santa Marta.

In Peru, a nine-hour trip from Lima to Huancayo, a mountain city known for its colorful market. This train travels higher than many small planes, climbing to an altitude of 15,700 feet before starting downhill.

And, if it's rain forest you want, try the 400-mile rail safari from Santa Cruz, Bolivia to Corumba, Brazil.

Hardcore rail buffs can save money by getting an Amerailpass, a ticket good for unlimited travel in nearly every country in South America. A one month pass costs $50, two months $75 and three months $90.

Unlike the Eurailpass, this ticket is sold in the countries in which it is valid, not in the United States.

I was anxious to get out of Chile before the presidential election of September 4, 1970. There were rumors that all hell would break loose if Salvador Allende won because he was a Marxist. I made it by two days.

Allende won by a narrow margin but nothing happened immediately. Three years later, however, on September 11, 1973, he was deposed in a right-wing coup. That same day, Allende was found dead of a gunshot wound. Although some people believed he was murdered, an international forensics team confirmed in July 2011 that his death was a suicide.

After Machu Picchu, I made my way through Lima to Ecuador and flew back to the U.S. from Quito. There was no reason to visit Colombia. I'd been there several times.

I made one side trip from Quito by bus to a town called Santo Domingo de los Colorados, where some of the Indian men had their hair painted red. There were hardly more than a dozen of them standing around.

I'd never try to dissuade anyone from going anywhere or seeing anything, but considering that the bus ride through the mountains on narrow, twisting roads lasted three hours each way, that little excursion was definitely borderline.

Except for a couple of colds and an occasional upset tummy, I survived South America in good health. At a restaurant on my last night in Quito, I figured I'd go wild and eat the salad.

By the time I arrived in Miami the next afternoon, food poisoning or something just as nasty had kicked in. As I went through customs, my gut was grinding and I was sweating profusely. Since I had also grown a beard in South America, I must have looked like a very nervous druggie.

The customs agent looked carefully through everything in my suitcase. When he came to a small plastic bottle containing a white powder, he said, "Aha, what's this?"

"Laundry soap."

He unscrewed the cap, took a big sniff and sneezed.

I made it back to Chicago shortly thereafter. It was a week before my tummy was back to normal. I definitely should have skipped the salad.

Norway

A cruise that went somewhere

Sandwiched between trips to more exotic locales, I spent a few months in Europe in the spring of 1971. The highlight was a cruise on a Norwegian coastal steamer.

Norway's Coastal Steamers
Landlubber's Delight

If you could reach onto a map and straighten out Norway's wrinkled coastline, it would stretch all the way from the northwest corner of Russia across the Atlantic to southern California, a distance of roughly 12,000 miles.

The general contour of the coast, however, measures less than 1,700 miles. The difference is the sum of 150,000 islands, countless peninsulas and half a dozen great fjords that penetrate inland for 100 miles or more.

It's easy to see why the shortest distance between two points is often over water and why coastal steamers remain the number one means of transportation along these rugged shores.

The main steamer run is a 2,500 mile, 11-day circuit linking some 40 ports between Bergen and Kirkenes, a small mining town near the Soviet border. The route is shared by the Bergen Steamship Company and four other lines. Operating 13 ships on a joint schedule, they provide one sailing each day.

Although the primary purpose of the steamers is to cater to local needs by carrying passengers, freight and mail from port to port, they also serve as excellent tourist vehicles. In fact, there's no better way to see the majestic coast and isolated fishing villages that so typify Norway.

The Bergen Line's brochures warn potential customers not to expect cruise ship luxury, but thanks to Scandinavian cleanliness and efficiency, most people wouldn't find much to complain about.

Actually, the steamers are a landlubber's delight. Since they rarely leave sheltered waters, there's a continuous panorama of scenery and a noticeable lack of rough seas. And if the ships do hit a rough spot, they're large enough – about 275 feet long – to plow through without pitching around much.

Using the ships as floating hotels, tourists can explore most of Norway without the usual inconvenience of repacking and finding a different bed to sleep in every other night.

There couldn't be a more fitting departure point than Bergen, a city that's easy to love despite its rainy climate. Bergen somehow manages to be old and new at the same time. It's one of those rare places where there's little clash in architecture even though some buildings date back 700 years.

High-gabled wooden warehouses built during the 14th and 15th centuries line part of the harbor, forming a picturesque backdrop for the fishing boats that sail in each morning to supply the waterfront market. Flower vendors add dashes of color as oilskin-clad fishermen wrap up lobster, cod or herring for Bergen's housewives.

Winding cobblestone streets lead from the central shopping area to parks, museums and medieval churches. Two mountainside parks provide magnificent views of Bergen and the islands that shield it from the North Sea.

A coastal steamer sails northward from Bergen every night at 11 o'clock. During the peak summer season, each ship carries a special courier whose job it is to assist round trip passengers and escort them on shore excursions.

One of the first ports of call the next day is Ålesund, an important fishing center with an exceptionally colorful harbor. In late afternoon, there's a four hour shore excursion that includes a bus ride along the coast from Molde to Kristiansund, a town built on three islands. Passengers rejoin the ship following dinner at a Kristiansund hotel.

The second day finds the ship docked all morning at Trondheim, Norway's second-largest city. There are shore excursions here on both legs of the trip. Trondheim is known for its huge 12th century cathedral, regarded as one of the finest ancient churches in the country.

Early on the third morning, the ship crosses the Arctic Circle. A line painted on coastal rocks marks the exact spot. Later in the voyage, King Neptune shows up in the first class restaurant to initiate passengers into his realm.

The farther north you go, the more barren and spectacular the landscape gets. At one moment, the ship might be sailing in the shadow of a towering cliff that seems to rise vertically from the sea. The next, it'll be threading its way through a maze of low rocky islands. Sometimes the waterways are so narrow, you could almost jump ashore if you wanted to.

Stops on the third day include Bodø and Stamsund. Like many isolated Norwegian towns, Bodø is surprisingly cosmopolitan. Its luxurious new SAS hotel houses a modern shopping center. Stamsund grew up around a fish processing plant that has an almost overpowering odor.

Part of the fourth day is spent at Tromsø, where there's an optional excursion to a 1,380 foot high cable car terminal from which you can see the entire area.

On the fifth day, the ship visits Hammerfest, which claims to be the northernmost city in Europe, then sails past the North Cape, a stately promontory facing the Arctic Sea. If weather permits, there is a shore excursion to the cape and a nearby Lapp camp.

On the sixth morning, the ship reaches Kirkenes, where it remains for little more than an hour before heading back to Bergen. The timetable is reversed on the homeward voyage, enabling passengers to see what they slept though on the northward run.

One of the highlights on the return trip is an overland shore excursion between the ports of Harstad and Sortland.

Passengers who don't want to sail back to Bergen can catch a southbound plane at Kirkenes.

The steamers try to be as punctual as possible. Two young Australian women on my ship, the *Nordnorge,* learned this the hard way by nearly being left behind at one small port.

One of the girls had a watch that was

running 10 minutes slow. They returned to the dock just as the ship was picking up steam about half a mile out in the harbor. Luckily, the courier noticed them and asked the captain to stop. The girls, meanwhile, found an old fisherman who happened to be sitting in his boat. They jumped in, handed him a fistful of coins and pointed frantically at the ship.

Passengers, wondering why the ship had stopped, assembled on deck to watch the old man's boat draw alongside and see the red-faced girls from Perth climb quickly up the rope ladder.

First class fare for the round trip voyage, including meals, ranges from $160 in winter to $340 in midsummer. During May and the last two weeks of August, the price drops to $300, and in April and September it's $200. Only the May through August fares include shore excursions.

Many first class cabins are reserved for round trip passengers during the summer, but they're frequently sold out as far as six months in advance. You can work around this logjam by booking a second class cabin and eating in the first class restaurant. The cost is 10% less than the regular first class fare.

Only a few first class cabins have a private bath for which there's a surcharge of $60.

The highest second class fare is around $140 round trip, but meals and excursions are not included.

Meals are a real treat. The food is served smorgasbord style with dozens of tempting delicacies displayed on a long table. The only limit is the size of your beltline.

Budget travelers can save money by

riding deck class (sleeping in the second class lounge) and eating ashore.

If you don't mind not seeing the midnight sun, the best time to take the trip is in spring or fall when the ships are less crowded. The midnight sun is visible in Bodø from June 1 to mid-July, in Tromsø from mid-May to mid-July and at the North Cape from mid-May to August 1.

The voyage can easily be incorporated into a grand tour of Scandinavia. From Hammerfest, you can travel through Lapland to Helsinki by bus and train for as little as $25 in transportation expenses. The buses are modern and comfortable and they operate virtually all year round.

For more information, see your travel agent or contact the Bergen Steamship Company at 505 Fifth Avenue, New York, NY 10017.

There were so few passengers on my ship that everyone ate in the first class restaurant.

Many of the round trippers were elderly British couples. As the ship moved farther north, more and more Norwegians got on, proving it was the best way to get from one town to another.

Leaving the ship in Hammerfest, I traveled overland to Helsinki by bus and train. I saw few Lapps in Lapland. Most were filling up their station wagons at gas stations rather than herding reindeer. But I did see reindeer near the highway.

For what it's worth, getting to Hammerfest as well as Ushuaia, Argentina, earned me the distinction of having visited both the northernmost city in Europe and the southernmost city in the world.

My ticket for the one way second class voyage from Bergen to Hammerfest in April of 1971 cost $46.50, plus $10.58 for four evening meals.

I had a little windowless cabin deep inside the ship with a double bunk and a wash basin. The upper bunk was empty. The bathroom was down the hall.

The last time I checked, my trip could be duplicated for about $1,000 with private bath, meals not included.

My story did very well, being published in six Sunday papers. The people at the Bergen Steamship Company were so impressed they sent me a letter offering me a free ride. Unfortunately, that particular company no longer seems to be in business, meaning my long-delayed free ride is out the window.

However, other ships are still providing daily service up and down the Norwegian coast. I've always thought those steamers would be far more enjoyable for tourists than one of the huge cruise ships that sails to nowhere.

The beginnings

Inspiration

I've visited at least 100 countries over the years. It's hard to come up with an exact figure because the geography keeps changing. Yugoslavia used to be one country. Now it's six. Germany was two countries for a while. Now it's one.

There were several things that got me interested in travel. Part of the credit goes to the U.S. Army, which gave me a look at the outside world for the first time by sending me to South Korea for 16 months. While there, I traveled to Japan twice and Hong Kong once on space available military flights.

After leaving the army, my first job was writing national and international news for the UPI broadcast wire. That got me wondering what the people, places and things I wrote about really looked like: the Berlin Wall for example, Big Ben in London and the pope blessing the crowd from his balcony in St. Peter's Square, not to mention ancient sights such as the Parthenon in Athens and the pyramids in Egypt. I developed a strong urge to fill in the blanks.

I was also inspired by two classic books. One was *The Royal Road to Romance* by Richard Halliburton. First published in 1925 and still available, it describes how he decided to travel after leaving Princeton rather than starting a career as his classmates had done. The book relates his experiences as he made his way overland from Europe to Japan.

For his inspiration, right on page 2, Halliburton quotes from Oscar Wilde's novel, *The Picture of Dorian Gray*. Taking some poetic license, he condensed and streamlined what Wilde wrote:

"Realize your youth while you have it. Don't squander the youth of your days, listening to the tedious, or giving your life away to the ignorant and the common. These are the sickly aims, the false ideals of our age. Live!

"Live the wonderful life that is in you. Be afraid of nothing. There is such little time that your youth will last – such a little time. The pulse of joy that beats in us at twenty becomes sluggish. We degenerate into hideous puppets, haunted by the memory of the passions of which we were too much afraid, and the exquisite temptations that we had not the courage to yield to. Youth! Youth! There is absolutely nothing in the world but youth."

The cover photo of *Royal Road* shows Halliburton* posing in front of India's Taj Mahal, wearing a turban and standing with his hands clasped behind his back and his feet spread wide apart, reminiscent of the swashbuckling silent film star Douglas Fairbanks.

The other classic was a novel, *The Asiatics* by Frederic Prokosch. It chronicles the adventures of a young American who hitchhikes across Asia, beginning on the streets of Beirut and ending on the Vietnamese border with China. I didn't know it when I read the book but Wisconsin-born Prokosch had never been to Asia – he made it all up. Nevertheless, he sure had me fooled. Although first printed in 1935, the book has been reprinted in recent years.

I also admired the works of Robert Christopher, an expert on traveling cheaply. He published paperbacks titled *Around the World on $80, 1001 Ways to Save Money Traveling in Europe* and a third one about hitchhiking across the Sahara – something I haven't done yet. I found some of those books in the local library. I imagine they've been out of print for a long time.

* Halliburton disappeared at sea in 1939 at age 39.

Europe welcomes the lower classes

Until the 1950s, only wealthy Americans toured Europe, or anywhere else for that matter.

Airfares were expensive. Guidebooks advised aspiring travelers to stay at the London Hilton or the Ritz in Paris and pack proper attire for the cocktail hour.

Then two things happened.

In 1953, Icelandic Air Lines (now Icelandair) revolutionized transatlantic air travel by introducing cut-rate flights from New York to Luxembourg.

And in 1956 an ex-GI named Arthur Frommer published a book called *Europe on $5 a Day,* demonstrating that a European vacation was within reach of Americans who never thought they could afford it.

Frommer's title was a bit misleading though. The $5 covered only food and lodging. Everything else, including transportation, was extra.

But prices were incredibly low.

Back in the mid-60s when I first went to Europe, admission to Madam Tussaud's wax museum in London cost only 70¢, the ruins at Pompei 12¢ and a second class train ticket from London to Paris less than $15.

In Spain, the price of a one month third class rail pass was the equivalent of $16 in pesetas. Coincidentally, that was the same amount the blood bank paid for a donation. Some backpackers would go directly from the blood bank to the train station.

Adventurous Americans discovered that if they stayed in youth hostels and hitchhiked, they really could get by on a grand total of only $5 a day. Whereas Frommer's bargain hotel rooms were priced as high as $3, bunking in a hostel cost no more than 50¢. And of course hitchhiking was not only free, but an acceptable mode of travel in Europe.

Setting foot in Europe

I missed the first wave of cheap European travel in the 50s. But after getting out of college, doing a two-year hitch in the army and writing for UPI for two years, I was able to do it in 1964.

When I told my sister Lynn what I was up to, she decided to tag along for a while. She had been working as an X-ray technician at Good Samaritan Hospital in Los Angeles.

Living in Chicago, I dropped by the American Youth Hostels office on Clark Street to buy a hostel card and a handbook listing the location of every hostel between Iceland and Israel. The book contained useful facts such as numbers of beds, whether meals were served and, in some cases, how far the hostel was from the train station.

Next, I bought a one way ticket on Icelandic for a flight from New York City to Luxembourg for $167.80.

Lynn caught up with me in Chicago and we traveled to New York by Greyhound.

We first set foot on the Continent on Monday, September 28, 1964. We traveled together for a month through Germany up to Denmark, then down through the Netherlands to England, staying in youth hostels and hitchhiking as often as possible. As I had heard, hitching was very good for couples.

At the hostel in Hannover, Germany, we met a 30-something Australian woman named Helen Murphy who was heading to Berlin in her small panel truck. Peter Flynn, a tall, thin, blond guy who lived near London, was riding with her. Helen said we could tag along.

Germany had been divided between East and West three years earlier, and we had to drive along the autobahn through East Germany to reach West Berlin. On the way, one of the front wheels fell off the truck.

A convoy of East German soldiers stopped to see if they could help. They were dumbfounded. However, Peter, being a truck driver, figured out what to do. We had lost the wheel because the bolts had shaken off the hub, so he removed bolts from other wheels to refasten the one that went rolling away.

Once in Berlin, we found the hostels had no spare beds. But we were able to get into a refugee center that had long halls and simple rooms very much like a hostel. It cost less than $1.50 per day.

Berlin had the feel of an armed camp with U.S., French and British troops much in evidence, especially in bars.

Crossing through the Berlin Wall at Checkpoint Charlie, a walk around East Berlin showed the Communist side of the divided city to be very drab.

The four of us returned to Hannover, getting to the hostel just before closing time. The next day, Helen took off for Paris, dropping me, Lynn and Peter at the entrance to the autobahn heading to Denmark. There we separated, with Peter hitching by himself.

The visit to Copenhagen was marked by a lot of rain. Amazingly, we ran into Peter again just before he boarded a train to return home. He invited us to drop by.

Lynn and I next took the train to Hamburg. At the hostel, we met an eccentric American with a phony British accent who was driving an old London taxi, a big, black, square thing. He offered us a lift, which we readily accepted.

The three of us moved on to Amsterdam, where Lynn and I saw various sights such as Anne Frank's house and van Gogh's oils. After a day and a half, we rejoined the owner of the old taxi, heading for the medieval Belgian city of Bruges.

It was a long afternoon. We stopped several times because of engine trouble. At one point, the guy bought screws to bolt the generator to the motor.

Back on the highway, the engine made a loud noise and the car stopped. After waiting about two hours, a little yellow Dutch repair car called *Wagen Wacht*, similar to AAA, appeared.

The man looked over the taxi, then told us the camshaft was broken and we'd need a tow. He said whatever we did, we should *not* abandon the car.

After he left, that's exactly what we did. The three of us started hitchhiking together, snagging a ride on a truck back to Amsterdam.

Living like the Brits

Lynn and I took Peter up on his offer, taking a ferry across the English Channel, traveling by rail to the London suburb of Greenford, then riding a bus some distance, followed by a little walking. Fortunately he was home. We ate, talked, then crashed into bed.

Being there gave us a close look at how typical Brits lived. Peter was in a two story row house sandwiched in the middle of a block of homes. His mother was usually there too but she was off visiting a relative in Australia.

There was no central heating. Warmth was provided by a portable paraffin heater that was moved to whichever room was the center of activity, usually the living room where the TV was. The heater burned a pink liquid that was highly flammable.

Shortly before bedtime, the custom was to place a hot water bottle under the covers where the feet would be so getting into bed wouldn't be a total shock.

The very simple bathroom, which included a tub, was squeezed into one corner at the rear of the house. The kitchen, with room for a table and chairs, was an addition jutting into the back yard, one step down from the house proper.

The only hot water in the house came from a small instant heater above the kitchen sink. If one wanted to take a bath, the tub was filled one bucket at a time from the sink.

At the neighborhood pubs, which Peter seemed to

frequent every evening, I noticed the men were offering cigarettes to other people and no one smoked his own. I asked Peter if they were just being generous or counting each cigarette. He said, "Counting."

    Lynn and I alternated between taking it easy, trying to live a semi-normal life and riding the train into London for a first glimpse of Big Ben, Piccadilly Circus, Trafalgar Square, Charing Cross Road and other famous sights. We contributed to the food budget and helped clean the house.
    After 11 days, I saw Lynn off at Victoria Station. She was headed for the Lebanese capital, Beirut, where most of our family was living at the time.
    A few days later, I also left, catching a train to France. I spent the next four months traveling through France and Spain to Morocco, then halfway across North Africa to Tunis, where I caught a ship to Naples. I turned up in St. Peter's Square on New Year's Day 1965 to fill in one of the blanks – watching the pope bless the crowd, including me.
    After that, I continued north through Italy, then moved down through Yugoslavia to Athens, where I climbed around the Parthenon, then traveled through Turkey and Syria to Lebanon. With few exceptions, I stayed in hostels and hitchhiked.

Bedbugs & Sara

    Leaving London, I bought a ticket only as far as the French coastal city of Calais, but rumors of bad hitchhiking convinced me to stay on the train to Paris. It cost me $8.68 to get to Calais and another $5.70 to Paris.
    For my first night, I went straight to the student quarter along the Boulevard St.-Michel and landed at the dingy Hotel Diane for 12 francs ($2.45).
    I don't know if the place technically had bedbugs but I was bitten multiple times whenever I got between the sheets. It

was all right when I lay on top of the blanket, so I did that. Being cold was better than being a meal.

I had no idea how to say bedbug in French, so I kept my mouth shut in the morning and set out to find another hotel.

I went first to American Express to check for mail. As part of its services, American Express held mail for clients, even those who only carried its travelers checks.

As I was leaving, I noticed an attractive young woman walking toward me, well-built with long dark hair and a Mediterranean look.

She raised one hand and asked if I could read English. Although she spoke English well, she said she couldn't read it. She wanted me to read a letter someone had sent her. We went to a café. I read the letter to her, then helped her prepare an answer. I never did believe she couldn't read English.

Her name was Sara Peres. She said she was from Israel and had been working as a model in Tel Aviv and London.

Since I desperately needed a hotel, I asked about hers and wound up getting a room there. It was the Hotel Eden in the Temple-Republic area – the same price as the first one but without bugs. I moved my things as quickly as possible.

Sara said she was interested in working as an *au pair*, of all things, so we looked at ads in the *Herald-Tribune* and I helped her make some phone calls. I went with her on one interview and it was clear she considered herself far too good for such a lowly job.

I was in Paris for four days and saw all the major sights including the Eiffel Tower, the Arc d'Triumph, the flea market and Montmartre. Sara and I went together to the Louvre to visit Mona Lisa, Venus de Milo and the Winged Victory.

I never did figure out what she was doing in Paris. I wouldn't be surprised if she's still there, cornering guys at American Express and asking if they can read English.

A lift in Spain

Still leery of hitchhiking, I took the train all the way from Paris to Barcelona, the Mediterranean seaport in northeastern Spain. As a novice rail traveler, I mistakenly sat in first class and started talking with two Canadian girls before the conductor banished me to second class.

We reconnected when the train reached Barcelona and decided to travel together by regional train to a hostel in a coastal town called Arenys de Mar. The hostel, which looked as if it had once been a monastery, was a short walk uphill from a tiny beach. It was a huge building with long hallways and room after room containing a total of 260 beds.

There were plenty of English-speakers staying there – Americans, Brits, Irish, Scots and Australians as well as the two Canadians. One evening, two dozen of us packed into a little bodega to celebrate the birthday of a Scottish girl who was turning 21. Drinking wine, cognac and rum, it seemed as if we were all old friends.

It wasn't unusual to meet plenty of Canadians as well as Australians on the move in Europe. Most Americans seemed to be from California.

At one point, the people running the hostel said the women would have to leave for a night because they needed the space for a group of boys coming in. They all found rooms in a nearby hotel for nearly the same price as the hostel. They'd been lucky to get into the hostel in the first place. About half the hostels in Spain accepted only men.

Like France, Spain was considered a bad country for hitchhiking. But I got lucky in Arenys de Mar. An American guy from Los Angeles and I linked up with Frank and Angelo, first-generation Australians whose parents had migrated Down Under from Italy. They had their own car, a basic vehicle bought specifically for getting around Europe. We spent a week and a half together traveling inland to Madrid, then back to the coast before splitting up in Alicante.

Backpackers in Spain who weren't fortunate enough to have access to a car traveled by train. All carried the same essentials in a common plastic fishnet bag – bread, which was the closest thing to the fabulous French baguette; oranges, which were cheap and plentiful; and little wedges of French Laughing Cow cheese, which was lathered onto the bread.

After eating Laughing Cow a number of times in Spain, I haven't been able to look at it since.

Many backpackers also carried red wine in so-called bodega bags which they filled from a barrel in a wine shop. Those are the little bags that are held high above the head and squeezed to squirt a thin stream of wine into the mouth.

Hostelling

The size, quality and atmosphere of the youth hostels varied widely. A small hostel in the country might sleep as few as a dozen people whereas big city hostels often had several hundred beds with dozens of double bunks to a room.
German hostels were known for cold showers and regimentation. The Rome hostel was famous for theft.
The ones in Florence and Luxembourg City were very nice. The one in Algiers may be the dirtiest one I ever saw.
My all-time favorite was a three-masted sailing ship docked in Stockholm named the *af Chapman,* which slept 130. The vessel was built in Britain in 1888 and sailed between Wales and Australia more than a century ago. She has served as a hostel since 1949 and was still in operation at this writing.
Other notable hostels included one inside the medieval city of Carcassone in southern France and another inside the old city wall in Nuremberg, Germany.
The hostel in the Moroccan city of Tangier may have been the only one where young Americans openly smoked hashish, which was readily available. The hash was pressed

into what looked like a small brown hockey puck. Smokers would slice off a sliver with a pen knife, roll it into a ball the size of a pea, then place it in their hash pipes and enjoy. These were not hippies but clean-cut 20-something guys.

When checking in to a hostel, guests had to hand over their hostel cards. And in some areas, they had to do some work before their cards were returned. I had to sweep floors in Amsterdam and peel potatoes in Brussels.

There were disadvantages to hostels such as a curfew – usually 10 p.m. – and the fact that most were closed during the day between 10 a.m. and 4 p.m. – not very convenient when it was raining. Many were located on the outskirts of cities and it often took an hour of asking directions and riding buses and streetcars to find them.

I spent a lot of time and effort trudging to hostels only to learn they were full. Or I didn't make it before 10 p.m. and was shut out. In such a case, if I were really lucky, the person in charge would recommend a YMCA, a reasonably priced hotel or student quarters not far away.

The popular hostel in Nice on the French Riviera was full when I arrived, so I and others slept on cots in a tent. In Sorrento, Italy, the hostel was so crowded I had to sleep on two blankets on the floor.

Sleeping bags were prohibited but sleeping sheets were required. They were nothing more than a sheet sewn in the form of a sleeping bag. The aim was to keep the mattresses clean since sleeping bags presumably had been exposed to the outdoors. Some hitchhikers carried sleeping sheets. If not, they could be rented at a reasonable rate.

Big city hostels had a three-day limit and were often difficult to get into in summer, but they did take reservations.

In Switzerland and Bavaria, there was an age limit of 25. There was no limit elsewhere, but preference was given to those under 30 when the beds started filling up.

Most hostels served breakfast – bread, butter, jam, cheese, sometimes cold cuts, and bad coffee. Many offered an evening meal at low cost. I never drank wine until I stayed in hostels. I didn't like the taste. But that was the standard hostel beverage in Spain and Italy, watered down and served by the pitcher. If you were thirsty, you drank it.

During the day when the hostels were closed, university cafeterias were great places to get good, inexpensive lunches.

Since every person who stayed in a hostel had the same goal – to see as much as possible for as little as possible – there was a great camaraderie you couldn't find in a hotel. I was always running into travelers who had just come from where I was going, people who were eager to fill me in on where to stay or eat, what to see and other helpful hints.

Rules of the road

Although hitchhiking was free and common in Europe, it was seldom easy.

The hardest part was reaching a spot from which to start. You became an expert at reading city maps, figuring out which bus or streetcar would get you closest to a good launching point – the entrance to a major highway.

Sometimes two or three hitchhikers would travel together by bus from the hostel to the highway. Or several might arrive at the same place by coincidence. In either case, they'd split up in an attempt to catch a ride. Generally two men together didn't have a chance. But sometimes a driver would pick up two hitchhikers who had purposely separated.

There were times when we would play leapfrog. One hitcher would get a short ride, then the second one would pass him and wave. Later the first one would pass the second one.

Although it might seem exciting to someone who's never done it, the business of hitching can be as routine as going to work each day. Adventure is often outweighed by boredom, tedium and frustration. After spending an hour reaching a good spot on a highway and not getting a ride, you find yourself asking, "What am I doing here?"

There are plenty of bad days when you hitch for hours and only move a few kilometers. Or even worse days when you're forced to backtrack into the city because of heavy rain or a total lack of rides.

On the other hand, there can be days when you're incredibly lucky, like the times I got rides all the way from Stockholm to Copenhagen and Istanbul to Beirut.

One thing you can count on is that most lifts will be memorable. One ride in Germany had me aboard a truck delivering empty cans to a sausage factory in Zweibrücken. I've also ridden at 200 km an hour (125 mph) in a gull wing Mercedes on a German autobahn and traveled through Morocco in a truck that stopped to haul farm equipment and cattle from one place to another.

You never know when you'll meet someone extra nice. Heading to Oslo, Norway, I got a lift from a carpet salesman who took me to the suburbs. Since he wasn't going into the city, he dropped me off at an electric train station and gave me money to buy a ticket.

In western Algeria, a Canadian hitchhiker and I wound up in a little town together and were getting something to drink before moving on. A local man who spoke English started talking with us. He invited us to his home, where his wife and daughter loaded us up with cookies, bananas and oranges.

Back roads of Algeria

Hitching to the Algerian city of Constantine from a town called Setif, I was picked up by a jovial bearded man driving a truck loaded with blankets. Sharing the seat with him was a lamb. The man, who didn't speak English very well, took me to a restaurant in the city.

While he was talking with the owner about where I might stay, two young Frenchmen overheard the conversation and said I could bunk at their place.

Moments later, two other Frenchmen joined us and we all had dinner together. One of them paid for my meal. I didn't know who. Considering the reputation the French had for rudeness in France, their hospitality was a pleasant surprise.

At the end of the evening, I wound up in the apartment of one of the Frenchmen. While he was at work the following day, I washed some clothes in the apartment and later visited the public bath. When he returned, we walked around Constantine, going through the old quarter of the city known as the medina. We later met with another Frenchman and his American wife, then visited a museum where one of the other Frenchmen worked. It was almost as if I lived there.

Dinner was at the same restaurant as the night before, joined by the French-American couple and another French guy. Once again, someone paid for my meal.

I got another surprise the next day when I took off walking in the direction of Tunisia: two French soldiers driving by stopped and offered me a ride. They took me to an Algerian checkpoint and asked the police to get me a lift to my destination – Souk-Ahras, the last town on the main highway before the Tunisian border. I thought I had it made.

After 45 minutes, the police got me a ride all right, but it was in a car headed to a town called Tebessa, which was literally in the middle of nowhere about 100 km south of where I wanted to go.

By the time I figured out I was off course, it was too late to do anything. I decided to sit back, enjoy the ride and improvise when I got to Tebessa.

The car was a large, roomy Citroën. My chauffeur was a heavyset man with a black beard. He was accompanied by an attractive woman, presumably his wife. Both were dressed in white robes. The woman had a veil. Whenever there was any roadside activity, even one person walking toward the car, she quickly pulled it across her face. But when we were in open country, she removed it. I found it amusing that she didn't care if the infidel in the back seat saw her face, but it was off limits for Algerians to gaze upon.

About halfway to Tebessa, the man pulled up to a combination gas station/café saying it was a rest stop. Leaving my things in the car, he took me into the café and ordered tea for me, then left. I drank it quickly and tried to pay but he had taken care of it.

I rushed outside. The car was nowhere in sight. After a few moments of mild panic, my driver reappeared and said he'd be leaving in 20 minutes. Everything was fine.

Fortunately Tebessa was not far from the Tunisian border. It was raining when we arrived there late in the afternoon. A few short lifts interspersed with a lot of waiting got me through Algerian and Tunisian customs and finally into a town called Kalaa Djerda, which miraculously happened to be on a rail line that ran to Tunis, the capital.

The train left at 1:40 a.m., giving me about six hours to kill. I spent some of the time sipping tea in a café. Everyone was surprised to see an American. The tea was on the house.

After the place closed at 9:30, the owner's young son led me to the train station where some railroad employees invited me to sit by a stove in a back room as they played cards.

The train left on time with me sitting on a hard bench in second class. There were few other passengers. I probably got about two hours sleep before the train rumbled into Tunis at 8 a.m.

Since I had no Tunisian money to pay for the ticket, the conductor kept my passport. I left the station and quickly changed money, then paid for the ride – a bargain at $1.50.

Despite being thrown off course, my journey through Tebessa undoubtedly was far more interesting than a ride straight to Tunis would have been.

A small town in Macedonia

Hitchhiking was horrible in the former Yugoslavia. One of the worst days I ever had was in the southern province of Macedonia. I covered only 50 km one day while trying to get from Skopje to the Greek border. After numerous short rides and long waits, I wound up outside a little town called Negotino just as it was getting dark.

I didn't see any train or bus station, so I found what appeared to be the only hotel in town. After trying unsuccessfully to converse with half a dozen people, I got a room for the night, then went into the restaurant and feasted on salad, goulash, bread and wine.

It was January and very cold in my tiny upstairs room. There didn't seem to be any heat in the hotel, but the comforter was nearly one foot thick, so sleeping was great. The problem was putting a foot on the floor in the morning.

I bought coffee for breakfast and the owner threw in some fried egg and pizza. Then I paid the bill: $2.87 for the room and food.

I figured my luck couldn't possibly be any worse than the day before, so I walked back to the highway. After 10 minutes, a truck heading south stopped and a young couple got out. They happened to be from Arlington Heights, Illinois – the same town where I had attended high school – although I hadn't known them.

After talking for a few minutes, they discovered they'd left their passports in the hotel where they'd spent the night, 40 km back up the road. It was common for hitchhikers to put their passports and money inside the pillowcase for security, especially in hostels or dormitories, and that's what they had done.

Just as they crossed the road to head back north, a Greek in a shiny black car stopped. He was going directly to the border. My luck turned good as theirs went bad.

Asian odyssey

Taking a break

After traveling through Europe and part of North Africa for four and a half months, I arrived in Beirut on February 4, 1965, exhausted. In fact, I went to a doctor to find out why I felt wiped out. He said "early jaundice" and told me to pop some vitamins and take it easy.

That was no problem. There was no longer any need to hitchhike or get caught in the rain because Beirut was almost home. My parents as well as both of my sisters were there, at least temporarily, living in an apartment. Only my brother Ed was still in the United States.

My mother and sister Jane had moved to Beirut the previous summer to be with my father, who traveled constantly and usually stayed in hotels. The big move was an experiment to see what my mother thought of living overseas. Lynn had joined them in November from Europe.

My father had worked for many years as a field representative for General Motors Overseas Operations, which sold diesel locomotives to railways all over the world. Although he spent a good deal of time in Egypt and Iran, his territory stretched from the West African nation of Liberia to East Pakistan, which later became known as Bangladesh. One thing he did was turn up whenever a ship arrived in port carrying locomotives to make sure the rail workers got them up and running.

Jane was attending a high school associated with the highly respected American University of Beirut (AUB).

Lynn had found a job as an X-ray technician at the American University Hospital, where she quickly learned how to say, "Take a deep breath and hold it," in Arabic.

A few months after my arrival, at the end of the school year, my mother and Jane returned to the U.S. – experiment completed. Since my father traveled most of the time, Lynn and I had the apartment more or less to ourselves, with rent and utilities paid.

Lebanon had everything. A few miles north of Beirut was a glittering casino. A few miles to the south were nice beaches where people rented cabanas by the year. Up in the mountains to the east were villas where the very rich went to escape the summer heat.

Beirut itself was a great place before it was destroyed repeatedly during various Middle East conflicts, a lively, international city known variously as the Paris of the Middle East, the Oriental Riviera and the Banking Center of the Middle East.

The apartment was in a high-rise in a wealthy neighborhood known as Ras (West) Beirut, within sight of the Mediterranean. Not far away was fashionable Hamra Street, home to smart shops and cafés.

Residential streets apparently didn't have names. If someone wanted to take a taxi to the apartment, he would direct the driver to the building itself – in my case, the New Itani Building.

When I first arrived, Beirut had little streetcars similar to San Francisco cable cars traveling between Ras Beirut and downtown. Following complaints that the charming little streetcars hindered traffic, they were replaced by smelly French buses.

The other mode of mass transit was shared taxis, called *Service* (sehr-veece), which were cheaper than traveling solo. Taxi drivers would constantly cruise the main streets looking for fares, yelling, "Taxi?" If you wanted to share the cab, you'd say "*Service*." If the driver was more interested in snaring a single passenger, he'd keep moving.

The center of Beirut was Place des Martyrs, a long plaza lined with banks. At the foot of the plaza, which sloped gently downhill, was the *souk,* a busy bazaar where one could buy almost anything.

I didn't have to rough it when it came to food. There was a supermarket in the Hamra district stocked with items such as frozen ground beef from Denmark and Campbell's soup, all at reasonable prices.

Lebanese TV broadcast American shows in English with French subtitles across the bottom and Arabic down one side. Two of the programs I occasionally watched were *The Untouchables* and *Combat!* with Vic Morrow.

There were a number of theaters in the city showing the latest films. Within walking distance of the apartment was the Edison, across the street and uphill from AUB. Among the movies I saw there were *Lawrence of Arabia, Zorba the Greek* and *What's New, Pussycat?*

I occasionally dropped by the Phoenicia Intercontinental Hotel for a dip in the pool, using my father's pass. Frequent poolside visitors included the wives of foreign correspondents who were working in trouble spots such as Yemen.

My most unusual experience in Beirut was visiting a nightclub few Westerners could imagine. I accompanied several guys from Somalia, one of whom was a friend of my sister Lynn.

The club was in a quiet, dimly lit neighborhood quite separate from the tourist areas. Inside, nothing fancy. Groups of men in Arab robes sat around tables ordering liquor by the bottle while taking turns puffing on a *hookah* or water pipe, also known as a hubbly-bubbly. Each table had one.

All eyes were fixed on an attractive belly dancer in the center of the floor who glistened with sweat as she danced on and on, accompanied by a small group of musicians playing Middle Eastern drums and stringed instruments. It was the real thing – considerably more raw and inspired than anything seen in a fancy hotel.

The Alexandria scam

Since I stopped short of Egypt when traveling across North Africa, I made a special trip from Beirut to see the pyramids and other ancient attractions.

I sailed to the port of Alexandria on a large passenger ship of the Hellenic-Mediterranean Line. There were a number of other foreigners aboard who were traveling deck class, as I was, to save money. We slept on benches – no cabin, no bunk – for a one way fare of $13.

The ship left Beirut at noon on a Sunday and docked in Alexandria around two o'clock the next morning. Passengers who had nowhere to go in the middle of the night – more than a dozen of us – were directed to a room at the port where we could sit on benches and wait for the dawn. We were all planning to take the train to Cairo, 100 miles to the south.

A man dressed in an Arab robe came in to remind us that the first train left at 5 a.m., but the banks didn't open until 9. He pointed out that it was illegal to change money on the black market. He said he assumed no one wanted to wait an extra four hours to change money and miss the first train, so he would be willing to help by selling us Egyptian pounds at the official rate. It's possible he was just trying to be nice, but I doubt it.

Of course I and presumably others had picked up Egyptian pounds in Beirut where money from all over the world was bought and sold, often at bargain rates, by banks as well as money changers on the street. But the man had us in a bind. He might have been a customs agent and no one could admit having Egyptian money for fear of being arrested.

The problem was solved by changing just enough to cover the train ticket. But even that was probably enough to make the man wealthy over a period of time by selling dollars and other hard currencies he collected on the black market.

Valley of the Kings

Once in Cairo, there was no more slumming. I had planned my trip to coincide with my father being in town and staying at the Nile Hilton.

With his rental car, he drove me around to see the Sphinx and the pyramids at Giza as well as other sights. Like millions of tourists before me, I had my picture taken sitting on a camel in front of a pyramid.

My main goal was a trip south to Luxor to explore the Valley of the Kings. The 400-mile journey was made aboard a train that shaked, rattled and rolled for 10 hours.

Luxor was a dusty town on the east bank of the Nile that had been the site of the fabulous city of Thebes, capital of Egypt's Middle Kingdom, 4,000 years ago. Although the city was destroyed and most of the royal tombs plundered by the time the Romans took over in 30 BC, the crumbling remains were still magnificent.

I found a hotel and rented a bike to get around. More adventurous visitors could rent horses, donkeys or camels.

Like every tourist, I was constantly pestered by little boys selling fake scarabs and other trinkets.

The Valley of the Kings, across the Nile from Luxor, held more than 50 ancient tombs. At least half a dozen were usually open to the public.

The only tomb that survived relatively intact was that of Tutankhamon, the teenaged king who became popularly known as Tut. His tomb was partially ransacked soon after burial but promptly resealed. It remained undetected for thousands of years after that because the entrance was later covered by rubble from a nearby excavation.

Exploring the tomb was an eerie experience because it was the only one in which the mummy was still present. Others had been shipped off to the Egyptian Museum in Cairo.

Knowing something of the discovery added a great deal of interest to the visit.

A British archeologist named Howard Carter spent seven years looking for Tutankhamon. He found the tomb on November 26, 1922, just as his financing was about to run out. It was and still is regarded as one of the most spectacular discoveries in the history of archeology.

In his book, *The Tomb of Tutankhamon*, Carter said he was "struck dumb with amazement" when he thrust a flickering candle into a small hole leading to the first chamber.

"As my eyes grew accustomed to the light," he wrote, "details of the room within emerged slowly from the mist, strange animals, statues and gold – everywhere the glint of gold."

Standing just behind him, his benefactor, Lord Carnarvon, asked, "Can you see anything?"

"Yes, wonderful things," Carter whispered.

Working, briefly

Back in Beirut, I was employed for six weeks at a fledgling newspaper at a salary of $75 a week – not bad at the time, especially since I was living rent free.

There were 16 daily papers in the city, including the English-language *Daily Star*, which was quite good. A Venezuelan businessman decided to give the *Star* some competition, so he assembled a staff headed by Lebanese.

His paper was to be called simply *Beirut*. It would be an eight page daily. I was the editor of the inside four, the feature pages. An Englishman and an Indian were put in charge of the news and sports pages.

Staff writers included three very personable foreigners who were more or less stuck in the country.

One was a slim, 30-something man from New Zealand who was so proper he always wore a three-piece suit. He was married to a Lebanese woman and had failed to renew his visa. He feared he'd be arrested and jailed if he tried to leave the country, so he stayed.

There was also a middle-aged American woman. She had come to Beirut to visit her daughter, who had married a Lebanese, then decided to hang around.

The third person was an American woman in her 20s who'd been in the Peace Corps in Thailand. She was making her way back to the U.S. when she ran out of money in Lebanon.

Problems with production became apparent from the start. For a printer, the executives had hired a company that normally manufactured calendars. They used monotype instead of linotype, meaning each letter was set individually instead of a line at a time.

It took several days to get the first test issue printed.

I noticed the Brit and Indian were laying out their pages British-style and I was doing mine U.S.-style. When I pointed this out to the Lebanese, it was decided the paper would be U.S.-style. The Brit and Indian were not amused.

It looked as if the paper might be headed for disaster, so I bailed out and traveled back to Europe to see places I'd missed the first time.

I started by taking a Yugoslav ship to Greece, then traveled through Italy, France, Switzerland and Germany to southern Scandinavia, making my way back through countries including Austria and Turkey.

The highlight of the trip was the Greek island of Mykonos, where I and a biology teacher from Wilmington, Delaware named Dave spent much of our time enjoying the beach with three young women from Los Angeles.

The most enduring memory of Mykonos was the sight of crusty old Greek fishermen dressed in black sitting at sidewalk cafés, ogling the passing bikinis.

When I returned to Beirut two months later, I learned the paper had folded without ever hitting the streets. I was probably the last one to be paid. I felt sorry for my former colleagues who probably needed the money more than I did.

By bus to Baghdad

Beirut was the launching pad for the longest trip I ever made – through the Middle East, India and Southeast Asia to Tokyo, then back to the United States. It began December 3, 1965 and lasted nearly seven months.

Apprehensive was the best way to describe my feelings as I rode through the mountains of Lebanon in a car driven by a woman from the U.S. Embassy. She, along with a U.S. Air Force officer and a Lebanese man, were bound for Jerusalem. Through contacts in Beirut, I had arranged for a ride as far as the Syrian capital, Damascus.

As we headed into the unknown, I kept wondering, "What am I getting into?"

It was like stage fright. I felt like jumping out of the car, returning to Beirut and taking the first plane to Paris.

Two hours after departing, much of the uneasiness vanished when I was dropped off at a hotel to begin the business of traveling. The hotel was the Basman, recommended by someone in Beirut. The rate was $1.75 a night.

After eating a cheese sandwich I had brought with me, I asked directions at the desk and set out to look for the office of the Nairn bus company, which had services to Baghdad. Nairn had been in business since 1923. One of its most distinguished passengers was British mystery writer Agatha Christie, who rode with Nairn in 1928.

I found the office. It was closed.

In the morning, I returned and learned there was a departure at 1 p.m. with arrival in the Iraqi capital the next morning at 9, a total of 20 hours. I bought a ticket for 31 Syrian pounds ($7.75).

After wearing out my feet exploring the *souk* and the national museum, which had a good collection of items from the Roman days, I picked up my suitcase from the hotel and headed back to the bus office.

The trip didn't start well. As the bus arrived to pick up the passengers, it sideswiped a small truck. After everyone was aboard, the bus had to be pushed to get it started. But that turned out to be only a local bus. It took us across town where we switched to a much larger one that looked like an elongated Airstream trailer.

It was 3:15 by the time the battered silver machine rolled out across the desert carrying 20 passengers besides me – Syrians, Iraqis and Lebanese.

Two young Lebanese, a man and a woman traveling separately, spoke English, so I had someone to talk with during the rest stops. The woman was bound for Baghdad. The guy said he was headed to Kuwait to look for a job.

The trip was as rough as I had expected. As the bus moved slowly over the unpaved road, dust sprayed out behind it like the wake of a ship.

Just before sunset, we arrived at the Syrian customs post, a building that looked like a frontier fort in a cowboy movie. The only other building in the area was a restaurant where most of the passengers got something to eat.

Sleeping was almost impossible because the bus was so uncomfortable. As the ride progressed, my rear end felt as if someone was pounding it with a meat tenderizing mallet.

The bus stopped every few hours for a rest break, sometimes literally in the middle of nowhere. When that happened, the passengers fanned out in all directions across the wide open desert to relieve themselves, forming a giant circle. The women trekked much farther out than the men.

At 4:30 in the morning, we arrived at Iraqi customs. It was so cold I did most of my waiting inside the office, holding my hands over an oil heater.

I later wrote an article about the trip. Since I hadn't broken into the travel writing business yet, I never got around to sending it to any papers, although it appeared to be good enough to print. It languished in my files until now.

Nairn Bus
Better Than a Camel

Aside from traveling by camel, one of the least expensive and most memorable ways of getting around the Middle East is by Nairn bus.

Founded by Gerald and Norman Nairn, two brothers from New Zealand who served with British Forces in the area during World War One, the Nairn Transportation Company, Ltd. has been making daily runs between Damascus and Baghdad since shortly after Lawrence of Arabia chased the Turks out of Syria.

In the early days before there were any buses or well-defined roads, Nairn used caravans of open-topped cars. Each car was equipped with a red flag atop a tall pole so the drivers could find each other if part of the procession happened to drop out of sight behind a sand dune.

If the caravan lost its way in a blinding sandstorm, the drivers would sit out the storm, then travel in a widening circle until they reached the road again.

The service has improved somewhat since then but the sense of adventure hasn't been entirely eliminated.

Nairn has extended its routes, making it possible to travel all the way from Beirut to Kuwait on the Persian Gulf.

The old cars have been replaced by homemade buses resembling giant metal shoeboxes. Like a semi-trailer truck, the driver's cab is separate from the bus itself.

Each bus is a dull silver color and it's covered with dents, scratches and a fine coat of dust. The nearly opaque windows are tight enough to make them unmanageable, yet somehow the cloud of sand that swirls around the bus makes its way inside.

The roads are a little better these days. Although most of the 500 miles separating Damascus and Baghdad are covered by a thin belt of gravel, the first few miles at either end are paved.

Each bus carries about 20 passengers, depending on how many suitcases, mailbags and assorted boxes, crates and burlap sacks are packed into the rear end. The passengers sit in seats resembling canvas beach chairs.

Up front with the driver is a mechanic who finds something to tinker with at every stop.

The desert is all but uninhabited except for people who run small adobe restaurants that pop up along the road every three or four hours. The buses make a rest stop at each one so passengers can stretch and have something to eat if they wish. The standard menu includes shish-ka-bob with Arabic bread and a choice of beer, Turkish coffee, Coke or Pepsi.

Arab passengers demonstrate their hospitality by offering to share meals with foreign travelers, refusing to let them pay.

The trip is supposed to take 20 hours but it's rare when it's that quick. With all the stops and delays, it's closer to 24 hours.

The rest stops last up to an hour. There also may be a few unplanned stops when the engine quits. At the Syrian and Iraqi border posts, the stops can last up to two hours, especially when the driver has to awaken the customs agents.

Perhaps the best thing about the trip is the price. The one-way fare from Damascus to Baghdad is less than $8.

And even though the buses and roads have been improved since the days of Lawrence, the ride is still unforgettable.

The trip took 25 hours and I thought I'd never be able to sit down again. Looking back, it's hard to believe the road between Damascus and Baghdad wasn't paved at that time.

I found a reference to the Nairn buses running as recently as 1996 but they presumably are history by now.

The end of the line was a bus station on the edge of Baghdad. As I retrieved my suitcase, half a dozen taxi drivers offered me a lift for astronomical sums. Fortunately I noticed a combination tourist office/airline terminal up the street. I picked up some maps and got a ride in a special airport-to-hotel taxi that took me into the city at a good rate.

Baghdad was larger and more modern than I had expected. I was dropped off at the YMCA. My $2.25 room was big enough to walk around in and fairly clean. I had to go down the hall to use the bathroom but the water was hot.

After 12 hours of sleep and a hot shower, I was feeling like a human being again.

My next stop was to be the Iranian capital, Tehran, which lay roughly 450 miles to the northeast. I could have taken a bus directly there, but I had another plan. Not being fond of buses, I hoped to travel more comfortably and at no cost on the Iranian railway.

Since there was no rail line between Baghdad and Tehran, I would travel south through Iraq, then cross into Iran and catch a train at Khorramshahr, which was 585 miles from Tehran. Before leaving Beirut, I had written to an Iranian railway official my father knew well, asking about the possibility of a free ride.

I spent only one full day in Baghdad. On the second morning, I was walking to the train station to check on trains to the southern city of Basra when I spotted a building where one of my father's Iraqi acquaintances, a Mr. Jabr, had his office. I had tried unsuccessfully to get him on the phone.

When I popped in, he not only was there, but he knew of two men who were driving to Basra in an hour. A ride was quickly arranged. There was just enough time for me to pick up my suitcase from the Y.

Off I went with a Scotsman and a German in a VW, a few minutes before 11 a.m. As we headed south, the people along the road were some of the most primitive I'd ever seen, living in mud and thatched huts. The only pleasant sight was the Tigris River at sunset.

We arrived about 7 p.m. My companions checked into the best hotel in town, then dropped me off at a cheaper place where I got a large but dreary room.

Basra was a giant slum. There weren't any big attractions except for a copy of a Babylonian lion statue in the middle of a traffic circle. It was ironic that southern Iraq was said to be the site of the Garden of Eden.

The city was so dirty I didn't want to take a chance on a restaurant, so I ate food I was carrying with me.

Between fighting off mosquitoes in the hotel during the night and listening to people argue in the next room, sleeping wasn't easy.

U-Turn on the river

Basra was located on Shatt al Arab, a waterway formed by a merging of the Tigris and Euphrates Rivers. I had to travel farther south to get to a spot across the river from Khorramshahr. The men who had given me a ride said I could do that quickly and cheaply in a five-passenger taxi. But that proved not to be true.

After asking around, I wound up at what was called a bus station. The buses, however, were little more than large homemade station wagons, battered and dirty. My first ride found me squeezed into one of the vehicles with six Iraqis. My luggage rode on top with some goats as we headed down a straight road lined with date palm orchards.

The next ride was in a beat up old Pontiac.

After passing through a village of mud huts, I wound up at an Iraqi customs shack on the edge of the wide river. I had my passport stamped, then a grubby man wearing an eye patch who was sitting outside at what looked like a card table gave me a customs form to sign. He had filled it in for me in pencil using block letters and wanted payment for his services.

He offered me one U.S. quarter and a British sixpence as change for one dollar. After negotiating, he settled for my last Lebanese pound, worth 33¢.

A couple of men carried my bag to a small boat with an outboard motor. I got in. As we pulled away, I asked the driver, "How much?"

"One dinar," he told me. I started complaining it should be half that amount. He responded by turning the boat around and going back to shore.

A dinar was worth $2.80. I asked two customs agents who were playing checkers how much the ride should cost. "One dinar," they replied in unison without looking up.

I got back in the boat. The driver and I continued arguing as we moved across the river. Although I had a one dinar note, I didn't want to give it to him, so I handed him 750 fils (3/4 of a dinar) plus one dollar. That was actually worth more than one dinar but he kept yelling anyway. I never was any good at bargaining in the Middle East.

I finally made it to the other side of the river with a great sense of relief only to find I was not in Khorramshahr but 15 miles downriver in Abadan. After three more shared taxi rides, I arrived at the train station in Khorramshahr. The "quick" trip had taken most of the day. From what I saw, the city looked almost completely new – certainly a lot better than Basra.

I talked with the men in charge at the train station. They hadn't heard anything about a rail pass for me. But, by a lucky coincidence, they said the man I had written to in Tehran, Mr. Sabety, was due to arrive in the morning.

After eating dinner at the station, I was allowed to spend the night in quarters set aside for railway employees.

When I caught up with Sabety the next day, a free ride to Tehran was quickly arranged. He explained that he had been away when my letter arrived and no one in his office knew what to do about it.

During the day, I wound up accompanying Sabety and half a dozen other people to a rare event – watching a train-washing machine being assembled.

One of the railway officials, Mr. Dodberi, was traveling to Tehran late that afternoon to visit his family, so he and I boarded the train together. It was very clean and nice.

Although Sabety said we were supposed to travel first class, we started out in a second class compartment which we shared with a teenage girl and an elderly woman, both of whom were dressed in Western clothing. Veils had gone out of style many years before in Iran. Only in third class did the passengers wear robes.

After an excellent chicken dinner in the dining car, Dodberi moved me into first class so I could sleep, then he returned to second class. That struck me as odd.

My new roommate was an Iranian businessman who asked questions about the United States for about an hour and a half before switching off the lights.

The next morning, I rejoined Dodberi in second class. We watched the Nevada-like scenery slide by until we arrived on time at 11:30 a.m. in Tehran.

I had mentioned that I stayed in low-priced hotels, so Dodberi and I hopped into a taxi and he took me to a place with running cold water that cost $1.90 a day.

Tehran was littered and filthy despite having wide tree-lined streets as in Paris. There were lots of beggars and unshaven men. I also noticed quite a few men holding hands, something I'd only seen before in Turkey on a lesser scale.

There was a very nice department store named Ferushka Ferdowski that stocked items from all over the world. At the other extreme were countless peddlers on the streets selling nylons, chickens, bananas, toothbrushes, nuts, sweaters, etc. Of course, the most interesting spot in the city by far was the huge covered bazaar filled with millions of beautiful Persian carpets.

I stayed in Tehran for four full days. Two days would have been plenty, but I had to get a visa for Afghanistan, which was no trouble, and wait for Sabety to return so he could arrange another train ride for me.

Bumpy road to Afghanistan

My next destination was Mashhad, at the end of the rail line in eastern Iran, 578 miles from Tehran.

Another first class ticket was arranged and Sabety appointed a man named Mr. Eghtedar to accompany me. Although I insisted I could get along fine on my own, I was nevertheless grateful to have a guide and interpreter.

Leaving at 11:30 a.m., the ride lasted 19½ hours. It was a pleasant and comfortable trip. Eghtedar and I either read, looked out the window or discussed Iran. There were very few towns along the way and the landscape was barren.

In one respect, the Iranian trains were more comfortable than their European counterparts: first class compartments were limited to four people rather than six.

We pulled into Mashhad at exactly 7 a.m., just as the sun was beginning to warm up the chilled night air. The stationmaster was to help me find a ride to Herat, the biggest city in western Afghanistan. He hadn't come to work yet, so Eghtedar and I drank tea until he showed up at 8.

The stationmaster immediately got on the phone and came up with two possibilities. I could either travel by bus or oil truck. I chose the truck.

After waiting several hours at the railway rest house, a man in a jeep took me and Mr. Eghtedar to a garage where the truck was being prepared. Eghtedar spoke with the driver, a white-haired man who looked as if he might be too old to drive. It was decided I would pay him 300 rials ($4) when we arrived in Herat.

The truck was very much unlike a typical Middle Eastern vehicle. It was clean, shiny and in good condition.

At 2 p.m., we began the 200 mile journey with me and a young assistant aboard. The old man actually was a very good driver. His assistant was a small, unshaven guy in his early 20s. Neither spoke English.

We traveled through desert with mountains off in the distance on either side. The road was paved for the first few miles. Then it became a dirt path, fairly straight and level in most areas but occasionally turning into a washboard. The only time the going was really rough was when we had to cross dry river beds.

It was 8 o'clock and very dark when we arrived at the Iranian border. We were there for at least half an hour because we had to go to three different offices with our papers. One of the offices was about a quarter mile away, so the assistant and I borrowed bicycles to get there. It was good to stretch my legs.

The moment we crossed into Afghanistan, the bumpy road got bumpier. There was no gate and no shelter of any kind at the border, just a lone soldier standing in the middle of the road huddled in a blanket. He checked our passports.

A few miles farther, we reached Afghan customs, which consisted of twin huts on each side of the road. We were only there briefly. Inside one of the huts, the turbaned man who stamped our passports didn't have a desk. He did the processing sitting cross-legged on a Persian carpet. Before we left, three men with flashlights looked over the truck, presumably to make sure we weren't smuggling anything.

Not long after crossing into Afghanistan, we stopped at a small adobe house. The driver indicated in pantomime that it was meal time. We entered a room that was completely empty except for carpets and a lantern for light.

While the drivers were served a chicken dinner, I made peanut butter and jelly sandwiches with food I was carrying. The three of us had tea, then hit the road again.

Around midnight, we stopped at another roadside place. The driver indicated we were going to sleep there. Once again, we went into a room devoid of anything except carpets. There was already one man sleeping. The driver had a cot and blankets. His assistant had a homemade sleeping bag. Since I had no bedding, I was furnished with a thin mattress and one blanket. The blanket wasn't very clean but it was so cold I didn't care.

A short time later, another truck pulled in and a fifth man joined us.

It was so cold when I awoke at 6 that I remained curled up until everyone else got up an hour later.

Breakfast was fried eggs, tea and bread. I had tea and bread. I didn't know what the financial arrangements were. I never saw any money change hands and no one asked me for any. One reason I didn't eat much was because I didn't want to complicate the billing. Or mess up my tummy.

We took off around 8 and were at the edge of Herat an hour later. It didn't appear the driver was going into the city, so I paid him and started walking.

Herat had a storybook look. The road was shaded by palm trees and lined with an endless row of shops selling everything imaginable. As I walked, I was passed by dozens of camel and donkey caravans. Colorfully dressed people hurried about.

With the help of a teenaged Afghan boy who spoke English well, I got a ride to the Afghan Ariana Airlines office on a horse-drawn carriage known as a *gadi* – the principal means of transport.

The city had no paved streets and few large buildings

except for a huge mosque and a new Russian-built hotel/ restaurant near the airport. At the time, the Soviet Union and the United States were competing for the hearts and minds of the Afghan people by constructing highways and other public works projects. The Soviets concentrated their efforts in the north, the U.S. in the south.

Since Afghanistan was a rugged mountainous country with no railroads, I gave no thought whatsoever to traveling on buses that I imagined would be crammed with passengers and carrying chickens on top.

I would have liked to have stayed in Herat for a day or two but I learned I had a choice of either flying out that afternoon or waiting four days for the next plane.

There was another hitch too: I could fly only as far as Mazar-e-Sharif because the plane was fully booked from there. But since I could continue to Kabul the next day, I decided to do it. It would be good to get a quick look at Mazar anyway. The price was right – all the way to Kabul for $10.86, including airport taxes.

Outside the airline building, waiting for the free airport bus, were four young Peace Corps volunteers, two men and two women, who were going to the airport to meet other volunteers. They were stationed in Herat teaching English.

We rode to the airport together in a Russian-built bus over a Russian-built road past the Russian-built hotel. The two-mile long road from the airport to the edge of Herat was the only paved road in the area.

The volunteers seemed to be enjoying their stay in Afghanistan. I asked if they often came across Americans traveling through Herat. They said they saw them occasionally but were reluctant to make contact because many turned out to be freeloaders. They were especially embarrassed by one bearded American who turned up at their school to take up a collection for himself.

A short hop on Afghan Ariana Airlines, which was run by Pan Am, got me into Mazar after dark. I took the Russian-built bus to the airline office in town and arranged to fly on to Kabul the next morning, then hopped into a *gadi* and asked for "the hotel." The driver took me to a large, plain looking building where I got a room for 77 afghanis, the equivalent of $1.10. I'm not sure "the hotel" had a name.

I walked around the area until the winter cold forced me back to the hotel. Like Herat, Mazar was dominated by a large mosque. The town seemed smaller but more built up.

Using bread I had brought from Tehran, I made a peanut butter and jelly sandwich.

The tub in the adjoining bathroom looked tempting, so I talked to one of the clerks and found out a cold water bath was free but hot water would cost 44 afghanis (62¢). I figured I could afford it even though the bath was more than half the price of the room.

The clerk lit a wood fire under the nearby water heater. When I filled the tub, I was surprised to discover the water was so dirty I couldn't see the bottom. But I got in anyway, not wanting to waste my 62¢.

In the morning, I had a few minutes to walk around before reporting to the airline office. Mazar was centered around the mosque, which was one of the biggest I'd ever seen. Most of the other buildings were either new or under construction.

Among the few people on the streets at 8 a.m. were women dressed in *chadris,* the Afghan shroud that covers every part of the body except the feet. Not even the eyes were visible. Their view of the world was filtered by an oval-shaped piece of heavy embroidery sewn into the *chadri.* The ladies looked like walking bowling pins.

Kabul and the Khyber Restaurant

Arriving in Kabul, the airport bus deposited me at the Kabul Hotel, regarded as the best in town. I went in and asked where I could find a cheaper place. The clerk suggested the Ariana, so I went there and again got a room for 77 afghanis.

The room was big and cold and had three beds. When the time came to sleep, I checked each bed and found they all had dirty sheets. I summoned two clerks, showed them the sheets and demanded a clean set. They examined each bed, picked the one with the cleanest dirty sheets and told me to sleep there. That didn't make me very happy.

There was a wood-burning stove in the room. It cost extra to use, but it was getting cold, so I had one of the clerks build a fire. It burned out very quickly.

I learned there were only three hotels to speak of in Kabul: the Kabul and the Spinzar, both first class, and the third class Ariana. Of course, one could also get a bed in the bazaar for 50 or 60¢.

After several days of freezing at night and washing in cold water, I left the Ariana and moved to the Spinzar for a lavish fee of 240 afghanis or $3.38 a day.

The Spinzar was a high-rise in the heart of Kabul that looked as if it had just been built. The furniture was new and modern. Although lacking a private bath, the hot water in the sink was scalding and the radiator was beautifully warm – a dream situation for washing and drying clothes.

The biggest surprise in Kabul was the cafeteria-style Khyber Restaurant, which had been highly recommended by numerous travelers before I reached Afghanistan. Not only was it new, clean and a short walk from my hotel, but I could get a very nice meal for $1.50. My only bad experience was lemon meringue pie with spots of mold. But finding lemon meringue pie in Afghanistan was amazing in itself.

Kabul was more up-to-date than I had expected with tree-lined streets and new buildings going up everywhere. The seamy side was seeing really grubby men roaming the streets and fighting to get on buses. That made me glad I had taken the plane.

As in Mazar, adult women were covered head-to-toe by a *chadri*. Men seemed to wear anything they could get their hands on – a wild mix of turbans, hats, robes, jackets, vests, pants and footwear.

Like other cities in the region, Kabul had an extensive bazaar. Items that attracted the attention of foreign travelers included antique-looking rifles and swords, which may or may not have been authentic. Sheepskin vests were popular with tourists too although they smelled so bad no one could possibly wear one. (The leather was said to be cured with urine.)

I already had visas for India and Pakistan which I picked up in Beirut. I had hoped to travel to Pakistan through Afghanistan's fabled Khyber Pass, the trade route once trod by Alexander the Great, Genghis Khan and other notable conquerors. However, due to tensions between Pakistan and India, I learned that foreigners were permitted to travel to and through Pakistan only by air, not on the ground. So Pakistan was out.

I had to wait three days for the next plane to New Delhi because it only left on Thursdays. In the meantime, I arranged a ride to the southern city of Kandahar through the U.S. Agency for International Development. That didn't work out because the taxi I took to the AID compound ran out of gas on the way there and I missed the ride. I spent much of my remaining time roaming the city.

The first snow of the season started falling in Kabul the day before I was scheduled to leave, a reminder that it was only three days before Christmas.

Long day at the airport

It was still dark as I walked across the park separating the hotel from the Afghan Ariana office at 6:30 a.m. It had snowed during the night, then stopped, making everything white and beautiful. The only thing stirring was a pack of more than a dozen dogs making circles in the fresh snow.

The airport bus left more than an hour late. Just as we arrived at the airport, it started snowing again and the visibility was soon down to zero. Not even the plane sitting right outside the terminal could be seen. Meanwhile, passengers were checking their bags and going through customs.

On the bus, I met Ron Wills, a UPI business manager based in Tokyo who was visiting various bureaus, a genial guy dressed in a suit.

Wills had so much luggage, about half a dozen pieces, that the customs men wanted to inspect everything. Upon discovering six Afghan rifles and a sword, they got very excited and demanded to see an export permit from the Kabul museum verifying they weren't valuable.

A big commotion ensued when Wills said he didn't have one. He told me he hadn't bothered to get one because he never thought he'd be asked. He ended up leaving the weapons at the airport and phoning someone at the embassy to pick them up.

I had no idea whether the weapons were antiques. Wills probably didn't either.

At mid-morning, passengers began grumbling about being hungry, so the airline gave in and picked up the tab for everyone in the coffee shop.

Around 1 p.m., the hunger complaints mounted again. The airline reluctantly handed out sandwiches and coffee.

By mid-afternoon, the skies cleared and the passengers were finally allowed to board the plane. The pilot taxied to the end of the runway, revved the engines, then returned to the terminal. Engine trouble.

After hours of delays blamed on a fuel pump, the plane finally took off. At a brief scheduled stop in Lahore, Pakistan, it was a rough landing with the plane bouncing down the tarmac as the wheels hit first on one side, then the other.

When a steward came down the aisle, Wills asked, "What the hell kind of a landing was that?"

He replied: "The co-pilot was practicing."

I suspect that was one of the oldest airline jokes in the world but I'd never heard it before.

We finally arrived in New Delhi around 9 p.m.

I wouldn't say Afghan Ariana was the world's worst airline but it was definitely in competition. The flight lasted about five hours and there was nothing to eat or drink other than Coke and coffee, both of which disappeared quickly. The stewards explained that the sandwiches served at the airport to stifle a mutiny had been the food we were supposed to have eaten on the plane.

Adjusting to India

I spent four weeks in India, hitting New Delhi, Bombay, Madras and Calcutta, with a brief visit to Agra.

Starting in the mid-90s, the names of many Indian cities were officially changed to reflect local preferences, although the former names have not been completely abandoned. Bombay became Mumbai, Madras was changed to Chennai and Calcutta was revised to Kolkata. For this book, I'm sticking with the names in effect when I was there.

Arriving in New Delhi two nights before Christmas, 1965, I checked into a $3 private room at a YMCA. Almost immediately, I was hit with a really nasty case of the flu and could barely move for a week. The 50 degree temperature difference between Kabul and New Delhi may have had something to do with it.

On Christmas Day, I was still aching all over, so I left the room only for meals and to buy a newspaper. Christmas went virtually unnoticed in India anyway.

As my condition gradually improved, I forced myself to walk as much as possible to make good use of my time.

Before I arrived in India, everyone who had ever been there told me it was worse than I could imagine. India was so dirty that it was a surprise to find anything clean. The population problem was quite obvious. There were people, people, people everywhere, and it's amazing to think the population has more than doubled since then.

Nevertheless, my first glimpse of New Delhi made me feel as if I were back in civilization. Major streets were wide and everything looked fairly modern. The parliament and other government buildings were impressive.

Getting around either by foot or traveling in a two-seat motor scooter taxi, I visited places such as the bazaar, the Red Fort and the spot where Gandhi was cremated.

After a week, I decided to move on to Bombay, traveling by train and stopping en route in Agra to see the Taj Mahal. I paid my bill for six nights at the Y: 96 rupees, officially $20.42 but only $11.03 with black market rupees. Finding the black market was never a problem. It came to me. I was constantly approached on the street by money changers.

The train ticket to Agra was a real bargain: first class for only $2 at the illegal rate. I had gone to American Express and asked for a ticket to Bombay with a stop in Agra. The clerk said, "I cannot do that. You must buy one ticket from here to Agra and another from Agra to Bombay."

That sounded strange but I figured he knew more about it than I did.

The train ride was very comfortable in an open car with airline-style seats. I had the feeling the car was designed for foreign tourists because it was more luxurious than the regular first class coaches. I spent most of the three-hour trip talking with a Rice University physics professor and his wife.

As soon as we got to Agra, I went to the information desk to find out about buying a ticket to Bombay.

"Young man," the clerk said. "There's a six-day waiting list for that train."

He said it would be faster to return to New Delhi and take another train.

I suddenly became angry with the guy at American Express. He did tell me it was possible to catch the Bombay train in Agra but neglected to say it was highly unlikely.

I'd been the victim of a trick perfected by the Indians. When an Indian answers a question, he gives only the most basic, simple answer. He never volunteers anything that might be helpful. The visitor must ask a direct question to get a direct answer. The clerk in New Delhi knew I couldn't move on from Agra but didn't tell me because I hadn't asked.

Shocking Agra

Expecting beauty in Agra, I was shocked to find the train station as well as most of the city was filthy and crowded with dirty people. Agra was by far the most money-grubbing place I'd ever been.

Pedicabs and a few horse-drawn carriages followed me everywhere. Six pedicabs were on my tail when I left the train station and started walking toward the city center. I was able to convince all but two that I didn't want a ride. I even crossed to the other side of the street to discourage them but they moved over and traveled against traffic.

After another half mile, one of them gave up. But the remaining driver continued following me chanting, "Rickshaw, rickshaw."

When I stopped to look in the window of a souvenir shop, a man came up to me and pointed at the persistent pedicab driver. "This man would like to know if you want a ride," he said.

"Tell him he's so obnoxious I'd never ride with him."

I resumed walking and the pest soon disappeared.

Although the Taj itself was full of "guides" and child beggars, that didn't dim the fact that the white marble mausoleum was an incredible sight, as was the Agra Fort a short distance away.

One nice thing about Agra was discovering a restaurant chain called Kwality, where I was fairly certain I could eat a meal and not experience tummy trouble. The emphasis was on ice cream but a wide variety of meals was also available. There were branches in every large city.

I returned to New Delhi, once again talking with the professor and his wife on the train. Then I took a taxi to the Y, got my old room back and collapsed.

The next day, I heard the same old story on the trains. First class was booked for days but I could show up at the station and take my chances at grabbing a seat in second class. That was enough to convince me to abandon my plan to travel by surface as much as possible and fly to Bombay.

Using black market rupees, I bought a ticket on Indian Airlines for $26.65. That was five times what the train would have cost but quicker and easier on the nerves.

The plane was a Caravelle. The flight was pleasant.

New Year's in Bombay

Once in Bombay, the driver of the Indian Airlines bus went out of his way to drop me at the Y. There, I learned I could stay only one night because all the rooms were booked for the next day. I wound up in a large room with four beds. My roommates were one German and two Indians.

The next morning, the desk clerk suggested I try a hotel run by the Salvation Army called the Red Shield. I was leery because I suspected it might be something like a homeless shelter, but I found it, checked it out and decided to stay. Similar to the Y, it was a place accommodating a large percentage of foreigners who were traveling cheaply.

And it *was* cheap, less than $1.50 a day using black market rupees, meals included. And the meals were good.

My roommate was a thin, proper British civil servant named G.W. Tame. He worked for the government of Hong Kong, was on holiday and about to travel to England by bus.

The overland journey was supposed to have originated in New Delhi, but due to the border skirmishes between India and Pakistan, he had to fly to Karachi and board the bus there. The overland India-UK trek was popular among travelers with a lot of time, a sense of adventure and a cast iron butt.

It was New Year's Eve. After eating at the Red Shield, G.W. and I, joined by a young Australian guy, put on neckties and went across the street to a fancy hotel called the Taj Mahal Palace to take part in whatever festivities were planned.

Bombay was a "semi-dry" city, so we had to use our drinking permits to get a beer. The permits came with our visas. We had just finished downing a second mug of beer in the crowded bar when, moments before 11 p.m., waiters and police started hustling everyone out. We were amazed that the bars would close at the usual time even on New Year's Eve. But this was India.

We stood on the steps of the hotel watching as throngs of revelers with noisemakers and firecrackers jammed the street. After getting tired of repelling beggars, we returned to our room and were asleep by midnight.

In November 2008, the Taj Mahal Palace was attacked by terrorists, resulting in more than 160 deaths, including many tourists.

I spent two and a half more days in Bombay exploring the city. The weathered buildings with wooden shutters looked older than those in New Delhi.

I considered traveling next to Goa, a longtime Portuguese enclave far to the south of Bombay, but I realized I couldn't go everywhere and see everything.

Goa had been under control of the Portuguese for 450 years until India decided to kick them out in 1961. At the time I was in India, Goa was a haven for hippies. Nowadays the main industry there is tourism, with European vacationers attracted by the beaches, the colonial architecture and the East-West flavor of the place.

Hot and grubby Madras

Ultimately, I decided to fly to the southeastern city of Madras, having given up on traveling by rail. Once again, it was very cheap thanks to the black market: $24.33.

After a flight of less than two hours, I was there. The airport bus dropped me off in the city center, then I took a taxi to the YMCA only to find it was full. I had heard men might be able to stay at the YWCA, so I went there by pedicab and found out it was true.

The building, on the outskirts of the city, resembled a villa. My room was truly Maughamesque. There were bars on the windows – no glass, just shutters – plus a ceiling fan and a mosquito net draped over the bed. It was far better than the YMCA, which appeared to be quite dirty.

There was an interesting mix of guests. One evening, an American guy pulled out a ukulele and started playing. For the next two hours, virtually everyone staying there gathered around, listening and occasionally singing – two American girls, one British girl, two British women, one Australian woman, two Indian women and one Japanese girl. That demonstrated one of the benefits of traveling – getting to meet fellow travelers as well as the locals.

Out on the streets, the level of poverty was beyond belief. Many children were naked or nearly naked and many adults were in rags.

Bombay had been hot and humid. Madras was worse. The people were much darker than those up north thanks to the blazing sun. The stifling humidity encouraged older stone buildings to develop patchy black crusts.

The city itself, the architecture, was very impressive but, as elsewhere in India, there were people everywhere. The only plus was that there didn't seem to be as many beggars. But the ones who did hassle me were real gems, like the leper with a black hole where his nose should have been.

Madras was supposed to have a nice beach, so one day I went there to sit in the sand and watch the waves roll in. The beach was all but deserted, but as soon as I sat down, six boys and a man appeared out of nowhere. Three little boys wanted money, another tried to sell me a soft drink and two others just stood and watched. The man was a pedicab driver trying to solicit my business.

After 15 minutes, I left. With my feet aching, I decided to use the pedicab man who had been pestering me. Knowing it was wise to set the price in advance, I asked how much he wanted to take me to a train station near the Y.

"It's up to you," he said.

"If it's up to me, I won't pay you at all," I joked.

I held up a one rupee note and said, "This is what I'll give you. OK?"

He patted the seat and repeated, "It's up to you."

The train station was about a mile away. When we got there, I stepped out of the pedicab and handed the driver the rupee.

"One rupee," he screamed. "This is …"

I was out of sight before he could finish. It must have been enough because he would have chased me if it weren't. I had no idea what the actual fare should have been.

I was never trying to cheat people like him. It was all a game. The pedicab and taxi drivers were always trying to squeeze as much money as possible out of foreigners while budget travelers like me were trying to spend as little as possible. I suspect the pedicab guys scored big on occasion. That's why they glued themselves to foreigners.

I wanted to visit Ceylon (later renamed Sri Lanka), the large island off the southeast coast of India, so I spent quite a bit of time researching how to get there.

One person told me there used to be a train connecting with a ferry to the island. But he said it didn't run anymore because a bridge near the boat terminal had been washed out by a cyclone the previous year. Another man said the cyclone also sunk the boat.

When I checked with the airlines – Indian and Air Ceylon – I was told there was a wait of at least 12 days for a flight to the capital, Colombo. In fact, Air Ceylon told me I could be 49th on the waiting list on the 13th day.

"Why the wait?" I asked.

"Oh, the big Indian tourist season."

I thought there might be someone intelligent working in the TWA office, so I went in and asked if everything I had heard was true.

"Yes," the man said. But he had another idea. There was a roundabout way of getting there by taking three planes – first to Tiruchirapalli, south of Madras, then to Jaffna on the northern tip of Ceylon and finally down to Colombo.

I thought I had it made. I rushed back to Air Ceylon. The man confirmed it was possible but said there was an eight day wait!

I gave up, went to Air India and bought a ticket to Bangkok via Calcutta and Rangoon. Since it was an international booking, I had to use real money: $117.80.

Of course, I could have saved by flying to Calcutta with black market rupees, then buying an international ticket there, but I was so frustrated I hadn't thought of it.

Oh, Calcutta!

Arriving in Calcutta, I rode into the city on the airport bus with an American named Ken who was on the same plane.

We wound up in different hotels but it turned out both of us had tummy trouble that evening and neither had eaten much of anything all day except the food on the plane. I had assumed the Indian planes were a refuge from bad food. Apparently not.

Both the Y and the Salvation Army were full, so I spent the first night in a nearby dump called the Astoria and moved to the Red Shield the next day.

After learning that Ken had come from Ceylon, I told him about the runaround I had experienced.

He'd been given the same 12-day wait story. But since he had an open ticket, he found out what time the plane left and went to the airport. There were plenty of empty seats.

Ken explained that the airline clerks had no idea how many seats were available, so they simply told everyone the planes were full. (Of course those were the days before computers.) He added that a few seats were always reserved for government officials who never showed up.

Having missed Ceylon, I was determined to get to Nepal. Preparation included getting a visa at the Nepalese Consulate in exchange for three ID photos and 10 rupees.

From what I saw of Calcutta, it lived up to its reputation as one of the dirtiest cities in India.

One day, Ken and I met a British guy who had been there for a few days. He offered to lead us to some of the hard-to-find sights such as the Temple of Kali.

After traveling by streetcar to the south side of the city and walking along a series of side streets, we were at the temple. Like everywhere else in India, the area was crowded with people. There was a line to see the statue of Kali, the Hindu goddess of death.

The statue was black, had six arms, bulging eyes and its tongue was hanging out. As people filed past, they paused, screamed, then tossed money at it. Kali was certainly hideous but I never got the urge to either scream or toss money.

Outside the temple, the streets were lined with shops selling pictures and statues of Kali and other Hindu gods.

A short distance away, we stopped by a burning *ghat*, a riverside area where Hindus were cremated. One cremation was beginning as another ended. The bodies were wrapped in white cloth and placed on a bed of wood, then covered with pieces of wood on all sides. It was somewhat disturbing to notice the head and feet sticking out, so we didn't stay long. The mourners left as soon as the fire started. Only the funeral workers stuck around for the whole ceremony.

Packed like sardines

I learned that one of the cheapest ways to get to Nepal was to take a train to Patna, a large city on the Ganges River, then catch a plane to Katmandu from there.

Buying the train ticket was easy for a change. It just took time. It was always necessary to stand in at least two lines to find out which line I should really be in. After a good hour, I had a second class ticket for $2.85.

I also tried to buy a plane ticket from Patna to Katmandu but Indian Airlines told me they could get me a confirmed seat only if I paid for a long distance phone call to Patna. I decided to leave and take my chances.

Traveling light, I left my suitcase in the care of the Salvation Army and packed a few things in an airline bag, then hopped on a tram to catch the 9 p.m. train.

Howrah Station, across the river from Calcutta, was very crowded. There were so many people lying or sleeping on the floor that it looked like an army field hospital after a major battle.

There already were quite a few passengers waiting on the platform. When the train pulled in 35 minutes before departure, there was a mad rush to get on. The first people aboard got the most prized spots – the luggage racks – the only place a person could really stretch out. The luggage itself went under the seats, between the seats or in the aisle.

I was the only one in the car who wasn't an Indian. Nearly everyone carried a giant sleeping bag – bags so big they overlapped here and there as people seized territory.

I was fortunate to get a seat without anyone sprawled over me. The seats were wooden and covered with a thin cushion. That seemed to be the only difference between second and third class. No cushion in third.

It took at least an hour before everyone got settled, and it was quite a sight. The sleeping bags were stretched out in all directions on the luggage racks, the seats, the floor and on top of piles of luggage. Needless to say, I didn't get much sleep but the 12-hour trip wasn't as torturous as I had expected.

When the train pulled into Patna Junction, I had no idea where the Indian Airlines office was, so I bargained with a pedicab driver to take me there.

I felt a twinge of panic when the airline clerk told me the plane was full and there were four people on the waiting list. But putting my newly acquired knowledge about Ceylon to use, I persuaded him to sell me an open ticket. I handed over a $10 travelers check and a $5 bill and got five rupees in change. (I had to pay with hard currency because it was an international flight.) Then I rode the airline bus to the airport.

My ticket was taken without hesitation, leading me to to believe there wouldn't be a problem. As it turned out, there were four or five empty seats when we took off one hour late.

We climbed foothills before the Himalayas rose beneath the plane like a huge wall. The mountains were green, then brown, then white with snow. Ninety minutes after leaving Patna, the plane skimmed over a valley of terraced rice paddies and landed outside Katmandu.

Refreshing Nepal

Since it was January, I expected it to be very cold but was surprised to step off the plane into a 60 degree day.

On the recommendation of the British guy in Calcutta, I found the Hotel Panorama and got a room for $1.65 a day. The price included a private bath with occasional hot water but no heat, meaning it was a bit frosty in the morning. The room was cleaner than anything I'd seen in India.

The only hotel in Katmandu with heat was said to be the deluxe Annapurna. Fortunately, the weather remained sunny and pleasant during the day.

I learned I also could have stayed at the Peace Corps hostel. Although much cheaper, it was more than a mile from the center of town.

The Panorama had an American on its staff, a tall guy in his late 20s from Seattle. He said he had offered to help the manager improve the hotel, and thereby improve business, so he was hired.

After getting a room, I had to find the black market. I assumed that, like India, I'd be approached by dozens of people on the street to change money. Not so. I walked around Katmandu for more than an hour and no one even noticed me.

Suddenly, I spotted a tall Bohemian-looking European coming toward me. I figured he must know where to change money, so I stopped him and asked.

"Yes," he said. "The old man at the Globe can change it for you. C'mon. I'll take you there."

I had heard about the Globe in Calcutta. It was a restaurant where all the beatniks and backpackers hung out. The food was cheap and there were inexpensive rooms on the second floor.

The old man wasn't there, so the European, who turned out to be from the Netherlands, took me to a bookstore and handed me off to a Nepalese boy. He led me through a maze of streets to a house where we sat cross-legged on the floor as he sold me some rupees.

Now that I had money, I dashed back to the Globe for my first meal of the day: coffee and a plate of buffalo fried rice (water buffalo, that is), the most popular dish among the foreigners. It was good.

The patrons at the Globe included Americans, Brits, Dutch, Germans and a couple of South African girls. Many had their own little hash pipes and sat around by the hour getting stoned. Some had been in Nepal for weeks and had hiked through the Himalayas. A few said they had walked to the Tibetan border.

I picked up quite a bit of local information at the Globe. Someone mentioned I could get a visa for Burma easily at the British Embassy, so I went there to check. It was true. The visa was issued immediately. It cost only 21¢ and no photos were required. The only problem was that it was a transit visa good for only 24 hours. The reason it was so easy was because Britain was authorized to issue visas on behalf of Burma since there was no Burmese mission in Nepal.

That put an end to a potential crisis in Calcutta, where I was told I couldn't buy a plane ticket to Burma without a visa and couldn't get a visa without a ticket. Now I had both.

Nepal was a refreshing change from India.

Katmandu was loaded with charm. The bazaar was full of colorfully dressed people who apparently had come down from the mountains to shop. There were Buddhist temples everywhere. Each evening at one of them, musicians gathered to play songs with flutes, drums and bells.

A couple of times I borrowed one of the hotel's bicycles and pedaled to villages and temples a few miles outside the city. With no one bothering me, it was very pleasant. The most interesting temple, two miles away, was called Swayarnbhunath, or the monkey temple. It was crawling with sacred monkeys, of course.

I had washed some clothes in the room the first day I was there and after three days they hadn't lost a drop of water. I mentioned it to the manager and he strung a line on the roof for me. Everything was dry in two hours.

One day I went shopping with a University of Washington professor and his wife. He bought some Nepalese hats. I picked up an 18-inch-long curved Nepalese knife for a scant 12 rupees – less than $2 even at the official rate.

One interesting shop was the Red Chinese bookstore which sold, among other things, North Vietnamese propaganda material and postage stamps. The most popular stamp among young foreigners was one that depicted a U.S. military helicopter being shot down. "Victory at Ap Bac," it was called. I had read about it in *Time* magazine.

I spent three full days in Katmandu. The American who worked at my hotel filled me in on the cheapest way to get back to Calcutta. I could take a plane over the mountains to a little Nepalese town called Simra, then catch a train just across the border in India.

Although I preferred traveling by surface, that flight was not a luxury. Using black market rupees, the ticket cost only $2.13, and a quick hop in a DC-3 was preferable to spending hours on a bus careening down treacherous mountain roads.

Two wild and crazy guys

I encountered the lanky Dutchman again at the Royal Nepal Airlines office as he and I both arrived to board the airport bus.

Once at the airport, a second Dutch guy appeared. He had lost his passport and spent the morning getting permission to leave Nepal and enter India.

The plane apparently hauled a lot of cargo. The interior was all scratched and the seats were stuck in holes in the bare metal floor. The only service was provided by a young man in a sport shirt and slacks who handed out candy.

Like *The Little Engine That Could,* the plane barely seemed to clear the mountains, but after only 20 minutes, we landed on a grass airstrip near Simra. From there, we traveled by airline bus to a Nepalese town on the Indian border.

On my arrival in Nepal, I had been handed a currency declaration form on which exchanges of money should be recorded. Since I hadn't changed any money legally, I was a little concerned about what I would do if customs asked for it. Fortunately, no one did.

Traveling with the Dutchmen, it took several hours to make our way to the nearest Indian train station, walking two and a half miles through Nepalese and Indian customs to a town called Raxual. There, for the equivalent of 35¢, we bought third class tickets to the next big rail junction, Muzaffarpur, then waited several hours to board the train.

It was then that my companions first amazed me with their bag of tricks. Since we were at the beginning of the line, they decided to reserve an entire car for us. One of them reached into his bag and pulled out a thick piece of chalk. On the outside of a car, in large letters, he wrote,

Special Car   Reserved   First Class

Once inside, they locked the doors and pulled down the window shades so no one could see in. It worked. Whenever someone came to the door, one of the Dutchmen opened it and turned the person around.

We had to change trains twice before we got to Muzaffarpur. There were no empty cars on the other trains but there was enough room for each of us to be comfortable. While waiting for one train, we used the time to grab some omelets in the station restaurant. Our destination was Patna, where I had flown from earlier.

After two more train rides, we arrived on the opposite side of the river from the city around 3 a.m. We followed the crowd and wound up on a large ferryboat. The Indians handed over tickets as they boarded. We had no idea where they got the tickets, so we decided to walk on as if we owned the boat. No one questioned us.

& Sometimes Hitchhiking

The ferry was a real museum piece. From the main deck, I could look down into the boiler room and watch sweating men shoveling coal into three red hot furnaces.

The ride took about an hour because we were upriver from Patna. When we landed at the boat dock, we learned that the train station was one mile away, so we decided to stay where we were until morning. We went into the first class waiting room where I tried unsuccessfully to get some sleep on the bottom shelf of a luggage rack.

We had traveled for nearly 12 hours on five trains and covered only 200 miles.

In the morning, we walked to the Patna train station and stashed our gear in the first class waiting room. The Dutch guys decided to get rail passes using phony student cards they had printed in Bombay. They had bought 100 cards and were selling them to fellow travelers to earn money. Since we were traveling together, they gave me one for nothing.

The cards were pink and said "University of Stockholm." There were lines to fill in the student's name and other information as well as a little square for a photo.

All long distance travelers carried ID photos in case they were needed for visas. I gave them one, which they glued onto the card. They also had a kit to make an official looking stamp to cover one corner of the photo.

With our fake student cards in hand, we boarded a train and rode to the next station to visit the railroad's business office. There, we found the appropriate official and filled out forms for the student discount, which meant we could buy a first class ticket for the second class price or second class for the third class price.

While we were talking with the official, the shorter Dutch guy put his elbow on the desk and made sure the man noticed his watch – something else from their bag of tricks. As the man expressed interest in the watch, the other guy and I left. He explained that they had bought a bunch of Timex watches in Kuwait for $4 apiece and were partly financing their trip by selling them to gullible people.

The bargaining must have been intense. It was nearly an hour before the Dutchman came out and reported selling the watch for 100 rupees. That was a little more than $20 at the official rate and a little less than $10 on the black market.

We returned to Patna. I bought a ticket to Calcutta and they bought tickets to New Delhi, then we split up. That was the only ticket I ever got with the student discount. Patna to Calcutta was a good 300 miles. I booked a first class sleeper. With the discount and black market rupees, it cost $2.82.

Although the price was right, getting the ticket required the usual rigamarole. The ticket clerk said he didn't know if there were any vacant seats on the train, but I'd have to buy a ticket in order to get on the waiting list. If there weren't any room, he said, I'd have to get a refund at one window before I could buy a second class ticket at another one. After some debate, I persuaded him to put my name on the waiting list and let me buy a ticket at the last minute.

First class was austere. I had two roommates in a four berth compartment, both Indian men. They had the usual giant sleeping bags. I had nothing, so I removed my shirt and covered my head with it. It was chilly but nice to stretch out.

I had no trouble getting a bed at the Salvation Army. I was in Calcutta for four full days, spending most of the time arranging the flight through Rangoon to Bangkok.

I had heard that Burma would pay room and board for passengers who used Union of Burma Airways both in and out of Rangoon, so I went there first. They made it as complicated as possible. They could get me a seat on any plane going to Rangoon but I'd have to wait six days for confirmation of a flight on to Bangkok. That was because there was no telex and they'd have to handle it through the regular mail.

Next, a smiling young woman at Thai International told me she could get me out of Burma as soon as I had a flight in.

I got a confirmed seat to Rangoon on Indian Airlines after cutting through the usual confusion. Although my ticket had originally been issued by Air India, the international carrier, it had to be rewritten by Indian Airlines, the domestic carrier, because the final destination was the Indian-administered Andaman Islands. I just happened to be getting off at an international stop on the way.

Burmese days

There were only four other passengers on the jet that took me from Calcutta to Rangoon on January 19, 1966. Arriving in mid-afternoon, it took an hour to get through customs – extremely long by international standards – because I had to fill out five or six forms and rummage through my suitcase to find a couple of ID photos.

The scrutiny at the airport, the difficulty getting into the country and the fact that my visa was limited to 24 hours undoubtedly had something to do with the fact that Burma was ruled by a wacko, xenophobic, repressive military dictatorship. The generals had taken over in 1962. They were still in power at this writing, nearly 50 years later.
Although the generals changed the names Rangoon and Burma to Yangon and Myanmar, much of the world still goes with the original names as a subtle form of protest.

Since I would only be there overnight, I left my suitcase with customs and went into the city carrying only my Pan Am bag, sharing the airline bus with one other tourist.
The bus went directly to the Strand Hotel, one of the great hotels of Asia. The stately Strand, which overlooked the Rangoon River, had been in business since 1901. With its Victorian architecture and high-ceilinged rooms, it was the kind of place Somerset Maugham might have stayed in, and he had.
The price of a bathless room was 48 kyats. The official exchange rate was 4.65 to a dollar, meaning the room was $10.25. I looked at the nearby Y and a place called the Green

Hotel. Although they were cheaper, I couldn't resist staying in the legendary Strand since it was so affordable.

I was standing on the sidewalk wondering where I could change money when a taxi driver fulfilled my wish. He drove me a few blocks then disappeared down a little street while I waited in the cab. When he returned, I traded a $5 bill for 75 kyats. At more than triple the official rate, that was the best black market deal ever – enough to pay for the room, dinner and breakfast and have change.

After registering and having a celebratory bottle of beer at the Strand bar, I took advantage of what light was left and visited the nearby Sule Pagoda, where an early evening Buddhist service was in progress.

Compared with the chaos of India, Rangoon was unbelievably quiet. It looked as if time had stood still since British colonial days. Much of the city had a rundown, seedy look. There were many cracks in the buildings and sidewalks. The grass in the parks could have been cut more often.

Rangoon was laid out well with wide, tree-lined streets. There was hardly any traffic though, and not many pedestrians either. The only crowds I saw were people gathered at a string of open air restaurants.

Despite the official coolness of the government toward foreigners, the people of Rangoon were cheerful and friendly, and most spoke English well.

Colorfully dressed women were smoking long thin cigars called cheroots. It was a national tradition much like Bolivian woman wearing bowler hats.

Betel nut was big. The sidewalks were stained with red splotches where people chewing the nut had spit out the juice that gave them a mild high. The habit was popular across an area from Pakistan through Southeast Asia to some islands in the southwest Pacific.

After dinner, I joined a British man and an attractive Australian woman in roaming the city until almost midnight. They were leaving at dawn, bound for India, so we tried to see as much as possible. That included walking around the outdoor food market where vendors were setting up for business early in the morning. On one side street, dozens of people were busy slaughtering ducks.

Breakfast was served in a large dining room packed with a planeload of European tourists. Except for moldy toast, the meal was fine.

Since I had a few hours before my plane left, I walked through the city to see the main attraction, the Shwe Dagon Pagoda, a sixth century building with a spire towering 368 feet above the ground.

The pagoda was on top of a large hill. I was surprised to see a modern elevator that took people to the top. The old-fashioned way of reaching the pagoda was to walk up hundreds of steps. There was a small fee to use the elevator.

I expected to find just one large pagoda and a couple of Buddhas, but there were dozens of pagodas in all shapes and sizes as well as thousands of Buddhas. I saw only a handful of people, mostly tourists. A few Burmese women bowed in front of the Buddhas and prayed while lighting candles and incense.

I had been handed a currency declaration form on arrival. Since the Burmese customs agents were so meticulous, I changed $2 at a bank and had the form stamped to make sure there wouldn't be any hassle when I turned it in at the airport. There wasn't. If questioned, I was prepared to say I had stayed at the Y. I bought cake and ice cream to use up the extra kyats.

Although I would have enjoyed seeing more of Burma, I felt I had accomplished something simply by being on the ground for 22 hours in what was essentially forbidden territory.

Bangkok: Oriental LA

Thai International was under the tutelage of SAS, and it showed. The Caravelle flying from Rangoon to Bangkok was so nice and clean it could have been on its first flight.

There was a Swedish pilot and a Swedish steward and half a dozen gorgeous Thai stewardesses wearing traditional dresses. Although no formal meal was served, the stews were in constant motion handing out sandwiches, coffee, cookies, oranges, wine, cigarettes and souvenir fans. Following weeks of grubbiness traveling through Asia, it was almost heaven – or nirvana in that part of the world.

After landing at Bangkok, I shared a limo into the city with a Swede and a Brit. A couple of former Peace Corps volunteers I had met in Katmandu had given me the business card of a hotel, the Suksawasdi, with the name and address printed in Thai, so I was dropped off there.

None of the hotel staff spoke English. I wound up in a large room with a double bed and cold shower for $2.50 a day. That was the real price. No black market in Thailand.

There was no air conditioning, just a three-speed ceiling fan above the bed that got a lot of use. The best thing was that the sheets and towels were changed every day, a definite rarity.

Bangkok struck me as an Oriental Los Angeles. Although there were no freeways, the city was spread out and the traffic was horrible. Bangkok and the Thais were a lot cleaner than anything in India or the Middle East and the people didn't make a habit of staring at foreigners.

Since the city was oppressively hot and humid, I was thrilled to see Foremost ice cream being sold, especially since a little Dixie cup cost only 5¢. I spent a good part of each day devouring the stuff.

Ovaltine seemed to be the national drink. It was made by pouring boiling water over a mixture of Ovaltine powder, sugar and condensed milk. It was available at little refreshment stands that sold drinks such as Pepsi.

There was a wide variety of restaurants in Bangkok, everything from Mexican to Hungarian. I often ate at places such as Wimpy's, home of the 25¢ hamburger; the Little Home Bakery and a pizza joint named Mario's. Restaurants serving Thai and Chinese food were everywhere. Thai food was inexpensive and very, very spicy.

When I was in college five years earlier, I'd known a student from Thailand named Wanchai Arthavedvoravudhi who attended for one semester. I decided to look him up, and found him.

Wanchai was doing very well professionally. He was the sales promotion director at Thai TV and had a company car with driver at his disposal.

He picked me up and showed me a house he was building, which looked like a home version of a Thai temple, then took me to dinner at a nice restaurant called Dukes.

Although I wasn't interested in staying in Thailand, Wanchai set up two job interviews for me. One was at an ad agency and the other was putting together newspaper supplements for $200 per month plus 10% of any ads I sold. Since I had no talent for sales, I backed out as diplomatically as possible.

I spent more than three weeks in the city. Using a bus route map, I was able to get around easily at 5¢ a ride.

There were enough museums, palaces, temples and other attractions to keep a sightseer busy for a solid week. There also were many good souvenir shops specializing in wood carvings, temple rubbings and Thai dancing masks.

Mailing souvenirs or anything else was remarkably simple. In the international section of the main post office, there were people who would wrap a box for shipping for as little as 15¢.

Detour to Vientiane

I wanted to visit neighboring Laos, which, like Vietnam and Cambodia, had been part of the former French Indochina, so I dropped by the Laotian Embassy and picked up a visa.

Leaving most of my things at the hotel, I headed north on a second class overnight train to Nong Khai, a town on the Mekong River 10 miles downstream from the Laotian capital, Vientiane. For a little while at the beginning of the trip, I was joined by a novice Buddhist monk, clad in a saffron robe, who wanted to practice his English.

Although the train was an express, the 500-mile journey took 13 hours, from 7:30 p.m. to 8:30 a.m. Sleeping was difficult despite the fact that the seat next to me was vacant.

After taking a pedicab to Thai customs, a boat across the river and a taxi to Vientiane, all for the equivalent of 80¢, I got a room at the Constellation Hotel, the only hotel I had ever heard of there. A basic room was 2,000 kip, or $2, and a meal in the restaurant $1, plus 80¢ for a bottle of wine.

I was too tired to do much the first day, so I rented a bike the next day. After an hour or two, I had seen the city.

Vientiane was very plain, very ordinary – no tall buildings, no tree-lined streets and no sidewalk cafés, although I had expected to see some because of the French influence. Most of the cars were either Jeeps or Citroëns. A good many people traveled on bicycles or Japanese motorbikes.

There were quite a few foreigners walking around. I assumed most worked for the embassies. The city was probably crawling with spies because Indochina was in turmoil as a result of the Vietnam War and the Pathet Lao, the Laotian Communists, were active.

I had considered traveling by bus on a twisting jungle road to the old royal capital of Luang Prabang, 250 miles to the north, but ruled it out because the Pathet Lao had been known to stop buses and rob the passengers.

About the only thing in Vientiane that might interest tourists were the Buddhist temples, but they were puny next to the ones in Bangkok.

Being a small out-of-the-way country, Laos did a good business selling large, colorful postage stamps to visitors.

Back in Bangkok, I made a side trip by bus to Pattaya, a beach resort about 100 miles to the south. Pattaya was just starting to develop as a travel destination because GIs fighting in Vietnam were using it as an R&R center. It was very nice but maybe not worth a six-hour round trip on the bus.

The bus to Angkor

My next destination was Cambodia. First, I bought a third class train ticket from Bangkok to Aran Prathat, where the rail line ended near the Cambodian border. Then from Air France, I picked up a ticket to get me from the capital, Phnom Penh, to Saigon. I also bought some Cambodian rials so I wouldn't have to change money right away.

The train ride, which cost only $1.17, took six and a half hours. Foreign passengers included one British man and a few Americans. There was a bus waiting that took us to Thai customs. From there, we walked half a mile to Cambodian customs. Then we waited an hour for a bus to take us to a town called Sisophon, where we switched to a connecting bus.

The countryside was very peaceful. Aside from occasionally seeing people working in rice paddies with water buffalo, there wasn't much activity.

The bus arrived in Siem Reap at nightfall. It was a nice looking city with a French atmosphere. A fellow American named Tom and I decided to get a room together. We went with some guys at the bus station who were recruiting for a hotel one block away and got a bathless double.

Siem Reap was the gateway to Angkor Wat, the 12th

Century royal temple that is one of the great architectural treasures of the world. It covers about 60 square miles and lies just a few miles outside Siem Reap.

The next morning, a waiter at a nearby restaurant showed us where to rent bikes. Tom and I spent that day and the next cycling around the ruins, sometimes together, sometimes separately. The ruins of course were fabulous. The tropical air was so heavy that if a smoker exhaled, the smoke would hang suspended in front of his face.

After two full days, we decided to move on to Phnom Penh, traveling once again by bus – a seven hour bone-jarring ride for 100 rials or $1.20.

Phnom Penh was much livelier and nicer than I had expected. We were only there for one full day. I tried to visit the Royal Palace but couldn't find the right entrance, if there was one, so I looked around a Buddhist cemetery instead.

I needed some Cambodian rials but no money changers approached me on the street. I didn't know what to do until I came up with the bright idea of finding an Indian. Passing an Indian dry goods store, I went in and asked. The man looked around to see if anyone was watching, then motioned me to the back room. Money was promptly changed.

Cambodia was incredibly cheap. An evening meal and half of a double hotel room each cost less than one dollar.

After nearly 48 hours in Phnom Penh, Tom and I flew to Saigon (later renamed Ho Chi Minh City), then split up.

Stranded in Saigon

It was February of 1966. Both the war in Vietnam and the anti-war movement in the United States were heating up. U.S. forces were conducting search and destroy missions in the jungles of South Vietnam as American planes pounded targets in the north. Hundreds of Americans and thousands of Vietnamese were being killed.

It was not the best time to be in Vietnam, but I was in Southeast Asia anyway and a guy I had served with in the army, Ray Herndon, was working there as a correspondent for UPI, so why not?

I arrived at Saigon's Tan Son Nhut airport early in the evening and headed for the city center where Ray lived with his wife Annie.

I hopped on an Air Vietnam bus for a ride through the chaotic streets to the airline's downtown office. There, I phoned Ray's apartment. Annie said he was in Laos but I should come over and she would help me find a place to stay.

Their apartment was on Rue Tu Do near the Caravelle Hotel. Tu Do was the center of activity in Saigon. The hotel housed many journalists and other international visitors.

I verified taxi prices at the airline office but all the taxis waiting outside wanted 10 times the normal fare. Then I noticed a *cyclo,* a three-wheeled bicycle that served as basic transportation in Saigon. The boy pedaling the *cyclo* agreed to take me to the Caravelle for 10 piasters.

When we got there, he refused to give me change for a 20 piaster note. I should have given him the 20 because it wasn't worth anything anyway, but I stubbornly asked for change from a cigarette girl standing nearby. While we were handling the transaction, I put my Pan Am bag between my ankles and squeezed tightly. I had to be careful because it contained my passport and money, among other things.

Suddenly I felt empty space between my feet. I spun around. The sidewalk was teeming with people going in every direction. My bag was nowhere in sight. I sprinted a short distance but soon decided it was hopeless. I returned to the *cyclo* driver, shoved 10 piasters in his pocket, then grabbed my suitcase, which I had naively left in his care.

After I found the apartment, which was a second floor walkup above a row of businesses, my luck improved. Annie, an attractive and personable Vietnamese woman, was having three people over for dinner. She invited me to join them. I not only had a good meal but met a UPI reporter named Martin Stuart-Fox who said I could stay at his place.

That turned out to be a three-story, four bedroom building he shared with three other journalists including his brother David, who was also a UPI reporter. Martin and David were from Australia. The third man was an American named Steve Northup, a UPI photographer. The fourth was Tim Page, a Brit regarded as a brilliant photographer.

Page, who had been wounded a number of times, was said to be earning several thousand dollars a week from *Life* magazine. The guys with UPI were probably lucky to be making a couple of hundred.

Tim's bedroom was on the top floor. Befitting his relative wealth, it was the only room with an air conditioner. The room served as something of a clubhouse for other journalists in town who would often gather there in the evening to relax and cool off. Most would smoke marijuana and debate which part of Vietnam the best pot came from. Danang was usually declared the winner.

I slept on an extra bed in a hallway.

The first thing I did on my first morning was go to the U.S. Embassy and report the theft of my passport.

Saigon was so crowded and dirty and chaotic that it reminded me of India. There were GIs all over, in and out of uniform. The sidewalks were lined with money changers, shoeshine boys and people selling items as disparate as newspapers and chipmunks, plus men pimping for prostitutes.

The streets were clogged with cars, motor bikes, motor scooters, bicycles and the ever-present *cyclo*s with their annoying drivers who asked disinterested foreigners over and over and over if they wanted a ride.

Since there was no American Express office in Saigon, I went to the Chartered Bank to see about a refund for my travelers checks. Although I had the serial numbers, I was told it would take three weeks.

I didn't want to wait that long, especially since American Express advertised instant refunds. At the UPI office, I learned that a local travel agency was a correspondent for American Express.

The agency was run by a heavyset Chinese man named Mr. Teng. His small, cluttered office was a place a film noir detective would have felt comfortable in. After I filled out the necessary papers, Mr. Teng said the refund would take about a week.

In the missing Pan Am bag was $470 in travelers checks plus $80 in cash. Other items included my camera – which was loaded with pictures of Angkor Wat – my light meter, a can of tuna, half a jar of instant coffee and half a jar of raspberry jam plus maps and tourist literature.

On my second full day, I checked with the embassy regarding the passport. It was there. I was told someone had found it in a trash can and handed it to an MP.

I had virtually no expenses except meals. Nevertheless, I had to borrow 1,000 piasters from Ray's wife the first day and another 2,000 from Ray when he returned the next day. All those piasters were worth less than $20, but they lasted for most of my stay.

Whenever I ate in a restaurant, I sat as far back from the entrance as possible because the Viet Cong occasionally parked bicycles outside packed with plastic explosives and blew off the front of the building. Most restaurants had iron bars covering the windows.

Shortly before my arrival, the VC had blown up a floating Chinese restaurant on the bank of the Mekong River. And while I was there, a bar was damaged by a blast.

Ray told me he was once walking along a sidewalk when a bullet smacked into a tree next to him.

I got the impression Martin Stuart-Fox and the other reporters saw more action than some of the troops. They were often up before dawn, heading to Tan Son Nhut, where they would jump into helicopters with soldiers and be ferried to a landing zone somewhere in the jungle. Sometimes they'd find themselves in the middle of a firefight. Sometimes there would be no contact with the enemy.

At the other extreme, less intrepid TV reporters were known to do their standups on the roof of the Caravelle Hotel.

One afternoon I was having drinks with a group of journalists alongside the swimming pool at the Saigon country club, known by its French name, the *Cercle Sportif.*

Most of the conversation was focused on one guy and a book his father had written. I had no idea who he was and we hadn't been introduced, so after we left, I asked. He was Sean Flynn, Errol's son. The book was *My Wicked, Wicked Ways.* Upon learning his identity, there was no question he bore a strong resemblance to his father.

After making some less than distinguished films in the early 60s, notably *Son of Captain Blood*, Flynn decided on a career as a photojournalist, so he turned up in Vietnam and did fairly well selling photos to the magazine *Paris Match.*

He disappeared in Cambodia in 1970 along with another photojournalist named Dana Stone. Neither was ever heard from again. Flynn was 29. Stone was 32.

At least twice over the years, remains were found that were thought to be theirs, but that proved not to be true.

Flynn and Stone weren't the only journalists I met in Saigon who were destined to become casualties. One evening at a party, I was introduced to Sam Castan, who was covering the war for *Look* magazine. Three months after leaving Vietnam, I read he'd been killed in a bloody firefight while traveling with the 1st Cavalry Division in the Central Highlands. Even though I'd only known him for a few seconds, it was sad to learn of his death. Castan was 31.

I'd been making daily visits to Mr. Teng to inquire about my refund, but nothing was happening.

Ten days after my arrival, the UPI bureau chief, Bryce Miller, returned from an overseas trip. When I told him of my predicament, he accompanied me to the travel agency, where he instructed Mr. Teng to send a telegram to American Express in New York saying UPI was holding a story about an American who was stranded in Saigon because he couldn't get a refund for his stolen travelers checks.

When we returned to the office, he also sent a message to UPI in New York asking the folks there to give American Express a call.

Three days later, UPI received a cable from American Express saying the money had been sent more than a week earlier to the Hong Kong Shanghai Bank. But no one had told anyone about it.

There was one more obstacle: I couldn't get the money right away because my passport was at the Vietnamese immigration office getting an exit visa.

But I was able to pick up both my passport and new travelers checks the next day. I immediately made a reservation to fly to Bangkok the following day and gave David Stuart-Fox about $10 in piasters to cover rent, Cokes and ice. After a goodbye dinner with Ray and Bryce and their wives, plus a few other journalists, I was ready to go.

I had spent 15 days in Saigon. If I hadn't been robbed, it probably would have been three or four. Because of the war, normal tourist activities were nonexistent. It was wise to be as inconspicuous as possible.

I wasn't the craziest person traveling around Southeast Asia. I later met a young Australian who had tried to enter Vietnam from Cambodia on his bicycle. The border guards reminded him there was a war on and turned him around.

To Singapore by train and taxi

After returning to Bangkok, I planned to make my way down the Malay Peninsula to Singapore by train, stopping at Penang, Malacca and Kuala Lumpur – a distance of more than 1,400 miles. First, I stayed overnight again at the Suksawasdi Hotel and did little more than wash clothes, grab a burger at Wimpy's and buy a ticket to Penang.

The next afternoon, I boarded a train for a 27-hour ride. I was stuck in a compartment with three other people, so the journey wasn't as comfortable as it might have been. But the fantastic jungle scenery made up for it. Outside the window, it was green, green and more green.

Penang is an island, so when the train got to the mainland city of Butterworth, I took a ferry across to George Town. The people at the Suksawasdi had recommended the Peking Hotel. I traveled there by pedicab and got a room.

Penang was one of the nicest places I'd ever been – very clean with an unhurried atmosphere. There were plenty of temples and nice beaches to visit. Grocery stores were full of U.S. products at decent prices. The only annoyances to contend with were the pedicab drivers.

Moving on, I spent one day in the Malaysian capital of Kuala Lumpur which was nice, clean and modern.

An American at the First National City Bank suggested I take a shared taxi when I moved on to Malacca, so I did.

I was interested in the city because it had been ruled for 500 years by the Portuguese followed by the Dutch, then the British. I ran around visiting old churches, forts and homes, but the city didn't have as much of a colonial feeling as I had hoped. Like the rest of Malaysia, it looked prosperous for an Asian city.

Again, I used a shared taxi to get to Singapore. The only problem was that I had to wait two hours for three more passengers to show up, but the three hour ride cost only $2. Although the taxis traveled faster than trains, the disadvantage was being stuck in one seat and unable to move.

In Singapore, I wound up by chance at the Chinese YMCA, which turned out to be quite satisfactory. I even had my own shower.

The city was more modern than I had expected. The downtown was very nice but the side streets with small shops were on the dirty side. Even then, it was against the law to spit on the sidewalk and people could be arrested for doing so.

Singapore was quite spread out. On Orchard Street, one of the main thoroughfares, there was a bowling alley. It had been a long time since I'd seen one of those. I also spotted a restaurant serving waffles. I hadn't seen one of those for quite a while either. I did have a waffle but I skipped bowling.

Aside from visiting the famous Raffles Hotel, the National Museum and the aquarium, which were all worth a visit, I spent much of my time planning my next move.

Singapore was a fork in the road. From there, I could either go south to the Indonesian capital, Jakarta, on the island of Java, or east to Borneo. I chose Borneo, the large island shared by Malaysia and Indonesia. The most rugged and underdeveloped three-quarters of the territory was administered by Indonesia. The Malaysian portion consisted of the states of Sarawak, on the northwest coast, and North Borneo, since renamed Sabah, on the northern tip of the island.

After visiting several shipping offices, I settled on the Heap Eng Moh Steamship Company and bought a ticket for the next sailing to Sibu with a stop in Kuching. The ship was the *Giang Lee*. My deck class ticket cost $9.35.

Kuching, capital of Sarawak, was a short distance up the Sarawak River from the South China Sea. It had been the headquarters of James Brooke, a British adventurer who set up his own little kingdom in 1841, becoming known as the White Rajah. Members of his family governed the area for 100 years, until the Japanese moved in during World War Two.

Sibu was farther north, about 40 miles up the Rajang River. It was the gateway for tourists who wanted to travel upriver to visit primitive tribes such as the Dayaks. I never gave any thought to that because I didn't think it would be fun to do it alone. Besides, I figured unless I mounted an expedition, I'd be shuttled through well-worn territory.

In both Sibu and Kuching, most of the people were ethnic Chinese.

Slightly upriver in Borneo

True to form, after I checked out of the Y in Singapore and went to board the ship, I was told it wouldn't sail until the next morning. I had to return to the Y. The new sailing time was 7 a.m. Actual departure was at 10.

We deck passengers were on the top deck at the rear of the ship. The area was covered with canvas that had flaps covering the sides. Everyone including me rented a cot rather than sleep on the deck. The sea was calm and the sailing was uneventful. I spent some time talking with a man who was heading for Kuching.

The Chinese lunch was horrible, so I dipped into my supply of peanut butter and jelly.

We arrived off the coast of Borneo between 3 and 4 a.m. on the second morning, then waited until sunrise to head upriver, docking outside Kuching at 9.

Kuching was bigger and better than I had imagined, although it was a far cry from a recent photo I saw showing skyscrapers all over. It had several good hotels, bookstores and even one snack bar where ice cream was sold.

I met a British soldier on the street who took me to the NAAFI to get something to eat. NAAFI stands for Navy, Army and Air Force Institutes – a British Forces combination PX/commissary/snack bar. That was a blessing because it was hard to find anything other than Chinese food in Kuching. After lunch, I joined him and three other soldiers for a few beers. I slept on the ship that night.

Kuching had several worthwhile attractions such as a museum, an old fort and the governor's house. After looking over those places on the second day, I returned to the NAAFI, ran into the same soldiers again, got something to eat, then visited the supermarket downstairs.

The ship was scheduled to leave at 4 p.m. But when I got back aboard, I learned it wouldn't be leaving until 6 a.m., so I went back into Kuching for ice cream.

The ship left promptly at 6 a.m. for a nine-hour voyage that took us along the coast again, then up the Rajang River. We stopped at two small communities, first Sarikei, then Binitang, where we spent the night. Both places were nice riverfront towns with shops and restaurants and services people needed – nothing exotic.

The next day, we arrived at Sibu, a town large enough to support an airport. I bought a ticket on Malaysian Airways to take me on to Brunei, the independent sultanate up the coast that occupied 1% of Borneo.

Brunei and Labuan

The capital of Brunei was Bandar Seri Begawan, although I never heard anyone call it that. The name Brunei seemed to apply to both the country and city.

The city was clean, orderly and nice looking but very small. I took my time walking around so I wouldn't see everything at once. I visited the giant mosque, where the custodian took me to the top of the minaret in an elevator so I could view the entire area.

I started out in a shabby hotel but on the second day managed to get a bunk in a four-bed room at the Hotel Brunei, the best in town. I had two roommates, both Chinese.

I wanted to see an island called Labuan, not far off the coast, so I checked out of the hotel and took a ship over on my second morning. Most of the passengers were Malaysian or Chinese except for a couple of British soldiers, one Gurkha (a Nepalese serving in the British army), and a German man.

I'm not sure the hotel I found could be classified as a hotel. My "room," directly above an Indian restaurant, was a thinly partitioned area with two beds and a table.

After checking in, I wanted to hit the beach, so I started walking and stumbled upon a British Forces swim club. I spent the rest of the day either swimming, sailing a small boat belonging to the club or drinking beer with a group of officers from a British submarine docked nearby. It was good to speak real English for a change.

    I later went aboard a Dutch ship that was headed for the Philippines to ask about a ride. The fare would have been about $50. Not bad. However, a man in the office looked up entry regulations and discovered they couldn't take me unless I had a ticket to leave the Philippines, which I didn't. I decided to continue moving north to Jesselton, the capital of North Borneo, a city since renamed Kota Kinabalu.

    There were no boats leaving Labuan on Sunday, so I had a boring weekend. Sunday was my fourth day there and I was anxious to move on.

    After bouncing back and forth between two offices Monday morning, I secured a ride on a 40-foot boat to the mainland, landing at a port called Kota Klias. It turned out to be a very small town with scarcely more than a dozen buildings, including a block of three or four stores.

    After a wait of only 10 minutes, a Land Rover taxi took me and two local men to a town called Beaufort, 12 miles up the road. Fortunately, Beaufort was the end of the line for a train that ran to Jesselton, 56 miles to the north.

    There was a train leaving soon but it was first class only, so I decided to stay overnight and travel third class in the morning.

    With the help of a British woman working as a teacher, I found the government rest house, which was very comfortable and cost only $2. I imagined British civil servants had similar accommodations during colonial days. After checking in, I walked around Beaufort for an hour. It was similar to other small Malaysian towns in that it had only two main streets with a few Chinese-run shops.

    Back in my room, I was thrilled to discover hot water and had my first hot shower since Nepal. I couldn't resist washing some clothes, then ate a canned meal in my room. Everything in Beaufort seemed to have closed at dusk.

The visa/ticket dilemma

I made it to the 6:20 a.m. train with seconds to spare and bought a ticket for $1.50. A few colorful backwoods characters got on and off as the train moved along, but most of the passengers were school children.

After finding a hotel in Jesselton which miraculously had hot water in the sink as well as a nearby shower, I concentrated on figuring out how to get out of Borneo.

Earlier, a travel agent in Singapore had requested a second class space for me on a Norwegian Asia ship sailing to Hong Kong. However, I learned that first and second class were fully booked and deck class had been discontinued.

I started making the rounds of travel agencies to look for another escape route. There were ships leaving for Hong Kong from the city of Sandakan on the other side of the island, but no one in Jesselton seemed to know anything about them, and I didn't want to travel there to find out I couldn't get aboard for some reason.

Then another problem cropped up. I received a bank check from home for $250. I was running short of money and needed to cash it but none of the banks, including big names such as the Hong Kong Shanghai Bank would touch it. They said they didn't have a record of the signature. I'd have to go to another country to get it cashed. Not an easy thing considering I was on an island.

I only had enough money to pay my hotel bill and buy a ticket to Hong Kong. But I couldn't do that unless I had a visa for Hong Kong. Remembering the trick I had to play to get into Burma, I found the office of the British Deputy High Commissioner and got a one year Hong Kong visa for $2. With it, I went to Cathy Pacific Airways and bought a ticket to Hong Kong via Manila for $126.

Meanwhile, I looked around Jesselton. It was clean and modern but there was nothing outstanding about it. There was a nice beach at Tanjong, three miles to the south, which I visited twice.

Bunking with the Peace Corps

The flight to Manila took an hour and a half. At the airport tourist office, I ran into five Peace Corps volunteers. Some were going to a PC hostel in Quezon City, the national capital outside Manila. I tagged along to see if I could get in.

The answer was yes. For two pesos (52¢) a day, I wound up in a seven-bunk room with two guys who lived there all the time. There was an adjacent bathroom with hot water and a kitchen everyone could use.

Cashing the $250 check continued to be a problem for a short while. Although neither First National City Bank nor Bank of America would touch it, American Express didn't even blink.

To escape the heat, people in Manila went to Baguio, a mountain community 155 miles to the north. I thought it might be fun to see the place, so I found the right bus and took off. The price for the seven hour journey was super – $1.30 – but the bus had wooden seats that were quite uncomfortable.

At an altitude of 5,000 feet, Baguio was certainly cooler than Manila because of natural air conditioning. The city was also much cleaner and quite pleasant because it was built on San Francisco-type hills. I spent some time roaming around a market looking at wood carvings. After overnighting at the Y, I was fortunate enough to catch an express bus back to Manila that took only six and a half hours.

I learned of a large passenger ship leaving for Hong Kong in two days, so I cancelled my plane reservation. Going to the Cathy Pacific office, I had my plane ticket signed over to the French steamship company, Messageries Maritimes. The price was virtually the same, around $55, but a ship was always preferable to a plane.

Before leaving, I wanted very much to see Bataan and Corregidor, two famous names from World War Two. They were located at the entrance to Manila Bay and I had to travel there by boat. Thanks to faulty information from the tourist office, I wasted one day showing up for a boat that wasn't at the dock. But I was able to recover by lining up a reservation for the next day on a hydrofoil.

Bataan is a peninsula that juts into the bay from the north, much like Marin County in San Francisco. It was the site of the famous death march in April 1942, during which Japanese forces prodded 75,000 captured Filipino and U.S. troops on a 60 mile march to a prison camp. More than 20,000 of the captives were either killed or died or escaped along the way. American dead were estimated at between 600 and 650.

After clearing the defenders from Bataan, the Japanese set their sights on Corregidor, a tadpole-shaped island to the south that sits in the middle of the opening to the bay. The well-fortified island had been a military prize for centuries.

Corregidor fell to the Japanese on May 6, 1942.

Most of the tourists on the hydrofoil were GIs. We stopped at Bataan for a quick look before landing at Corregidor. There we got a 90 minute tour. In addition to seeing old artillery pieces and barracks, the highlight was the Malinta Tunnel, which had been carved through rock by U.S. forces. It was 835 feet long, 24 feet wide, 18 feet high and had a little trolley running through it. The tunnel had been used as a headquarters as well as a storage area for food, ammunition and supplies. It was also equipped with a 1,000 bed hospital.

U.S. forces recaptured Corregidor in February, 1945.

Back at the Peace Corps hostel in late afternoon, I grabbed my things and headed for the harbor to board the ship. My bill for the hostel for six nights was astonishingly low – a grand total of 12 pesos or $3.12.

The ship was the *Laos,* a 532-foot vessel that carried more than 500 passengers. I was shown to my cabin, which was very small but nice. My roommate was a young Swiss guy headed for Japan. The meals were very good, especially baguettes and red wine for a change. My only complaint was that the air conditioning was too cold. I apparently had become accustomed to the tropics.

Amazing coincidence

One of the most amazing coincidences I ever experienced while traveling occurred on the ship. After boarding, I spotted a familiar-looking couple standing at the rail, watching the dockside activity.

I recognized them as Pete and Marge Mould, a Canadian couple I had palled around with in Egypt. We had met in Luxor. The last time I saw them, we waved goodbye outside the train station in Cairo. That was 14 months earlier!

Since then, I had spent time in Beirut and revisited Europe before taking off on my grand tour of Asia. Pete and Marge had traveled through Asia, renting a Land Rover to explore India, then worked for a year in Australia.

The odds of ever seeing them again must have been higher than hitting the lotto.

At home on the Star Ferry

The trip to Hong Kong took a day and a half. I spent much of the full day at sea reading.

Pete and Marge checked into a hotel called the Mandarin Guest House on Nathan Road in Kowloon. That looked too expensive for me, so I got a $1.58 room at the Y.

Since I'd been to Hong Kong before, I had some knowledge of the place. I felt right at home jumping on the Star Ferry for the 10 minute crossing between Hong Kong island and Kowloon on the mainland. The ferry was featured in *The World of Suzie Wong,* a 1960 movie starring William Holden and Nancy Kwan that made Hong Kong look dazzling while romanticizing the world's oldest profession.

I was there for five days, during which time I went to the China Navigation Company to check on ships to Taiwan. That was a Wednesday. There was a ship every Monday.

Only Chinese were permitted in third class, so I had to ride in second. But first, I was told, I'd need a Taiwanese visa. I got one from a place that looked like a travel agency. Then I bought a one-way second class ticket to Keelung, a port at the northern tip of Taiwan, for $26.30.

Nowadays, Keelung is often spelled Chilung.

Next, I picked up a visa for Macao, the tiny Portuguese colony known for its gambling casinos, which lies on the coast 37 miles southwest of Hong Kong.

I went there by hydrofoil and returned by regular ship. The hydrofoil took and hour and 15 minutes, the ship more than three hours, but it wasn't as cramped.

Macao was the first and last European colony in the Far East. The Portuguese took control in 1557 and gave it back to China in 1999. Since gambling was a major enterprise, I paid my dues by visiting two casinos and depositing $2.

The most beautiful reminder of Macao's past was the façade of the Cathedral of St. Paul, standing tall since 1602.

Pizzas in Taiwan

The ship taking me to Taiwan was the *Anking*. I shared a room with two other Americans: Gary Pruett, who was stationed with the U.S. Air Force in Taipei and James Boyd, a young missionary from Hong Kong. There weren't many passengers, so we had a six-bunk room to ourselves.

The third class Chinese were packed into much larger rooms, with some huddling around little portable stoves preparing their own meals.

I spent most of the time talking with my roommates and had to break out my supply of peanut butter and jelly to avoid the Chinese food. I don't dislike Chinese food but there's a big difference between what you get in a restaurant and what's served on a ship.

The trip lasted a day and a half, including a full day at sea. After docking and clearing customs, a man showed up to take James to Taipei, about 15 miles inland, so Gary and I rode along. Gary went to his base and I got a room at the Y.

Two things I noticed about Taiwan were that very few people spoke English and I saw few foreigners on the streets.

I visited three shipping agencies before hitting the right one and finding a ship that was sailing for Okinawa in three days. Before I could get to another office to reserve space on the ship, I was stuck at the Y for two hours because of an air raid drill. Relations were more tense than usual between Taiwan and mainland China.

The next morning, I was able to buy two tickets to get to Japan. First, to Naha on the island of Okinawa. There, I would change ships and continue on to Kagoshima, a city at the bottom of Kyushu, the southernmost of Japan's four main islands. The tickets cost $16 and $9.70 respectively.

Okinawa, a Japanese prefecture, is located about halfway between Taiwan and Kyushu. The island was captured by U.S. forces in the final land battle of the Pacific war, a battle that raged from April through June of 1945. It was governed by the American military until 1972.

I ran into Gary and James a couple more times and shared more beers, pizzas and hamburgers, not to mention using a washing machine in one of the air force barracks.

Sightseeing was done with a guy I met at the Y, a Peace Corps volunteer stationed in Thailand. Setting out in a light rain, we visited the Taipei history museum and the Confucius temple.

Slipping and sliding to Japan

To get to the ship, I had to take a bus to Keelung, where it was raining heavily. After the usual confusion, like being at the wrong end of the port, I found and boarded the ship, which naturally left four hours late.

Since it was a Japanese ship, there were no bunks, just large rooms where people could lie on the floor to sleep.

The only non-Japanese passengers besides me were one French guy and an American couple. The ship wasn't very crowded but the sea was rough during the night and the people trying to sleep on the floor kept rolling into each other.

At noon the next day, we stopped briefly at an island halfway to Okinawa and a large number of people got on. That evening, the sleeping rooms were so packed that the French guy and I slept on benches on the deck.

We arrived in Okinawa the next morning. Our little group of three Americans and one Frenchman decided to keep moving, so we shared a taxi to the next ship. At noon, after only three hours on the island, we were on our way again aboard a ship named *Okinawa Maru.* That ship was larger than the previous vessel, so it didn't rock as much. It was fairly crowded though. Instead of sleeping on the floor, I grabbed space on a large cushioned ledge along a wall.

It was windy the next morning, so I stayed below and read. We arrived in Kagoshima, a very pleasant city, early in the afternoon. A woman told the four of us where to find a bus to the youth hostel. We got there with no trouble. The standard overnight hostel fee was ¥250 or 70¢. I also had to buy a new hostel card because mine had expired.

That hostel didn't have the standard big Japanese bath, so they gave us free tickets to go to the public bath, which we used. Next to the cold showers at most European hostels, the hot Japanese baths were a luxury.

The French really know how to enjoy life. On my only full day in Kagoshima, my French roommate and I bought wine and cheese in a big department store, then took a ferry to an island in the bay and had a leisurely picnic sitting on the side of a volcano.

Hitching to Tokyo

I decided to hitchhike to Tokyo, so I shipped my suitcase to a major subway station, Shinagawa, then hit the road with a flight bag slung over each shoulder.

Hitching was fantastic because it was virtually unknown in Japan. Drivers were startled to see a foreigner standing on the side of the road. If the first car didn't stop, the second would. But it was always awkward because I spoke no Japanese and the drivers spoke little or no English.

One driver thought I was lost, so he turned around and took me to the train station in the city center. I had to make my way to the highway all over again.

Another driver asked for payment, which he didn't get.

Heading to Nagasaki, my last ride of the day was aboard an empty tour bus. When I asked a policeman how to get to the hostel, he stopped the passing bus and told the driver to take me there.

Somehow I got off the beaten track on my way to Fukuoka. I was walking along a country road when a teenage boy on a motorcycle stopped. Although he had a friend on back, he told him to hop off and insisted I get on, abandoning the guy on the side of the road.

It took more than an hour to get to Fukuoka. I was cold and hungry. The kid stopped to ask a man for directions to the hostel, then told me the man said I couldn't stay there. He didn't know enough English to explain way.

He said he'd take me to another hostel. Half an hour later, we arrived at a Buddhist temple in Fukuma, a town about 15 miles outside Fukuoka. It appeared I was the only guest. The fee was the same as the hostel. After the kid and I shared a meal, I took a bath and crashed.

The atomic bomb museum in Hiroshima was well worth a visit. All the displays and artifacts from August 6, 1945 – the day the city was vaporized – were well presented. There were melted Coke bottles and watches stopped by the bomb at 8:15 a.m.

At the end of the exhibits was a guest book for visitors to sign. I paged through it. Most people wrote things such as, "Shocking," Terrible" or "Never again."

However, one American man wrote, "Almost as good a job as Pearl Harbor."

The only problem I had with a hostel was in Kobe. When I tried to check in, the man in charge went berserk, saying foreigners weren't allowed to have Japanese hostel cards. That was untrue, of course. If it were forbidden, they wouldn't have sold me one in Kagoshima. The man said I could either pay extra or go somewhere else.

He was so nasty I didn't ask what "pay extra" meant. I left and caught a train to a town called Ashiya because there was a hostel there.

When I got to Ashiya, I asked a man in a shop to phone the hostel to verify it was open. The answer was yes but they told him it was too late to check in. Curfew was 9:30. It was 9:15. I guess they figured in travel time.

I wound up back in Kobe at the Y. It cost four times as much as the hostel but at least I had a place to sleep.

The date was Friday the 13th. I wonder if that jinxed everything?

Not far from Kobe, I visited Takarazuka, home of the all-woman musical theater revue featured in the 1957 film, *Sayonara*. I got into the park surrounding the theater for free because the performance had started and it was too late to buy a ticket.

I talked my way into the theater and watched 10 minutes of the four-hour performance, standing in back. It was lavish and colorful but I didn't have a clue as to what was going on because of the language difference, so 10 minutes was enough.

I continued hitchhiking, staying in hostels and seeing sights such as the temples at Nara and the giant Buddha at Kamakura, arriving in Tokyo two weeks after having landed at Kagoshima.

It was May 19, 1966. My big Asian odyssey was over. I found the hostel, picked up my suitcase at the subway station after paying an incredibly low storage fee of 50¢, then had an expensive pizza to celebrate.

When I learned the plane to San Francisco cost $435, I decided to return the other way, through Russia. It probably wasn't any cheaper but it seemed like a good idea at the time.

For $200, I bought a ticket at the Tokyo office of Intourist that would get me as far as Moscow. It was the same price whether I went through Siberia by train or plane.

The first leg of the journey was aboard a large ship sailing from Yokohama to Vladivostok. It was spacious and clean. The only problem I had was with the customs agents. When they came to my cabin to look through my suitcase, they tried to take my 18-inch Nepalese knife, insisting it was a weapon. I convinced them it was a souvenir. I still have it.

Unfortunately, there was no time to look around in Vladivostok, where a very comfortable train awaited us. It took the passengers north to Khabarovsk. There, many people transferred to the Trans-Siberian railway for a week-long journey to Moscow. I went to the airport.

Yes, I chickened out. I had decided in Tokyo that I'd fly. Although the Trans-Siberian was regarded as one of the great rail adventures in the world, I couldn't face a week on a train after traveling for nearly six months.

I had second thoughts about my decision after seeing how nice the train to Khabarovsk was. But I later learned from several people who had ridden the Trans-Siberian that it was not the same train; it was definitely in the roughing-it category.

After Aeroflot got me to Moscow, I traveled by train to Glasgow via London.

The most interesting thing about the rail journey was seeing the wheels changed at the Soviet-Polish border. It took a while to figure out what was happening when the train stopped and the cars were jacked into the air. The wheel assemblies were then rolled away and replaced with narrower sets. The Soviet tracks were a different gauge than the ones in Poland, so instead of having the passengers change trains, they changed the wheels.

One theory was that the Soviets chose a wider gauge so they couldn't be invaded by rail.

Home at last

From Glasgow, I flew to Chicago on Icelandic.

Once home, I wondered if I'd ever be able to find a job after spending so much time away. After all, it had been 21 months since I'd stepped off the plane in Luxembourg.

Luck was with me because I quickly got an interview at WBBM-TV. I thought the news director would be impressed with my travels.

Not exactly.

After I mentioned I'd seen much of the world, including trouble spots such as Vietnam, Cambodia and Laos, he said: "But what do you know about Chicago?"

"I was born here."

He hired me.

Footnote

The author has strong ties to Chicago. His maternal grandfather, William H. Lotts, was president and founder of Overland Construction, which did the steel work for a number of Chicago landmarks including the Tribune tower, the Board of Trade building, the Sheraton hotel and the sky ride at the Century of Progress exposition in 1933.

On the paternal side, his grandfather's first wife, born Minnie Hansen, was one of more than 600 people killed in the infamous Iroquois Theater fire on December 30, 1903. Grandfather Christopher Christophersen, who was a partner in a wood molding firm, later remarried and started a family.

www.ingramcontent.com/pod-product-compliance
Lightning Source LLC
Chambersburg PA
CBHW031246290426
44109CB00012B/453